World agriculture: towards 2015/2030

Summary report

FOOD AND AGRICULTURE ORGANIZATION OF THE UNITED NATIONS

Rome, 2002

Reprinted 2003

ISBN 92-5-104761-8

Foreword

This report summarizes the main findings of the FAO study, *World agriculture: towards 2015/30,* which updates and extends the FAO global study, *World agriculture: toward 2010*, issued in 1995. It assesses the prospects, worldwide, for food and agriculture, including fisheries and forestry, over the years to 2015 and 2030. It presents the global long-term prospects for trade and sustainable development and discusses the issues at stake in these areas over the next 30 years.

In assessing the prospects for progress towards improved food security and sustainability, it was necessary to analyse many contributory factors. These range from issues pertaining to the overall economic and international trading conditions, and those affecting rural poverty, to issues concerning the status and future of agricultural resources and technology. Of the many issues re-viewed, the report concludes that the development of local food production in the low-income countries with high dependence on agriculture for employment and income is the one factor that dominates all others in determining progress or failure in improving their food security.

The findings of the study aim to describe the future as it is likely to be, not as it ought to be. As such they should not be construed to represent goals of an FAO strategy. But the findings can make a vital contribution to an increased awareness of what needs to be done to cope with the problems likely to persist and to deal with new ones as they emerge. It can help to guide corrective policies at both national and international levels, and to set priorities for the years ahead.

The world as a whole has been making progress towards improved food security and nutrition. This is clear from the substantial increases in per capita food supplies achieved globally and for a large proportion of the population of the developing world. But, as the 1995 study had warned, progress was slow and uneven. Indeed, many countries and population groups failed to make significant progress and some of them even suffered setbacks in their already fragile food security and nutrition situation. As noted in the latest (2001) issue of *The State of Food Insecurity in the World*, humanity is still faced with the stark reality of chronic undernourishment affecting over 800 million people: 17 percent of the population of the developing countries, as many as 34 percent in sub-Saharan Africa and still more in some individual countries.

The present study predicts that this uneven path of progress is, unfortunately, likely to extend well into this century. It indicates that in spite of some significant enhancements in food security and nutrition by the year 2015, mainly resulting from increased domestic production but also from additional growth in food imports, the World Food Summit target of halving the number of undernourished persons by no later than 2015 is far from being reached, and may not be accomplished even by 2030.

By the year 2015 per capita food supplies will have increased and the incidence of undernourishment will have been further reduced in most developing regions. However, parts of South Asia may still be in a difficult position and much of sub-Saharan Africa will probably not be significantly better and may possibly be even worse off than at present in the absence of concerted action by all concerned. Therefore, the world must brace itself for continuing interventions to cope with the consequences of local food crises and for action to remove permanently their root causes. Nothing short of a significant upgrading of the overall development performance of the lagging countries, with emphasis on hunger and poverty reduction, will free the world of the most pressing food insecurity problems. Making progress towards this goal depends on many factors, not least among which the political will and additional resource mobilization required. Past experience underlines the crucial role of agriculture in the process of overall national development, particularly where a large part of the population depends on the sector for employment and income.

The study also foresees that agricultural trade will play a larger role in securing the food needs of developing countries as well as being a source of foreign exchange. Net cereal imports by developing countries will almost triple over the next 30 years while their net meat imports might even increase by a factor of almost five. For other products such as sugar, coffee, fruits and vegetables the study foresees further export potential. How much of this export potential will materialize depends on many factors, not least on how much progress will be made during the ongoing round of multilateral trade negotiations. Developing countries' farmers could gain a lot from lower trade barriers in all areas, not only in agriculture. In many resource-rich but otherwise poor countries, a more export-oriented agriculture could provide an effective means to fight rural poverty and thus become a catalyst for overall growth. But the study also points at potentially large hardships for resource-poor countries which may face higher prices for large import volumes without much capacity to step-up production.

Numerous studies that assessed the impacts of freer trade conclude that lower trade barriers alone may not be sufficient for developing countries to benefit. In many developing countries, agriculture has suffered not only from trade barriers and subsidies abroad but has also been neglected by domestic policies. Developing countries' producers may therefore not benefit greatly from freer trade unless they can operate in an economic environment that enables them to respond to the incentives of higher and more stable inter-national prices. A number of companion policies implemented alongside the measures to lower trade barriers can help. These include a removal of the domestic bias against agriculture; investment to lift product quality to the standards demanded abroad; and efforts to improve productivity and competitiveness in all markets. Investments in transportation and communi-cations facilities, upgraded production infrastructure, improved marketing, storage and processing facilities as well as better food quality and safety schemes could be particularly important, the latter not only for the benefit of better access to export markets, but also for reducing food-borne diseases affecting the local population.

On the issue of sustainability, the study brings together the most recent evaluation of data on the developing countries' agricultural resources, how they are used now and what may be available for meeting future needs. It does the same for the forestry and the fisheries sectors. The study provides an assessment of the possible extent and intensity of use of resources over the years to 2030 and concludes that pressure on resources, including those that are associated with degradation, will continue to build up albeit at a slower rate than in the past.

The main pressures threatening sustainability are likely to be those emanating from rural poverty, as more and more people attempt to extract a living out of dwindling resources. When these processes occur in an environment of fragile and limited resources and when the circumstances for introducing sustainable technologies and practices are not propitious, the risk grows that a vicious circle of poverty and resource degradation will set in. The poverty-related component of environmental degradation is un-likely to be eased before poverty reduction has advanced to the level where people and countries become significantly less dependent on the exploitation of agricultural resources. There is considerable scope for improvements in this direction and the study explores a range of technological and other policy options. Provided such improvements in sustainability are put in place, the prospects point to an easing of pressures on world agricultural resources in the longer term with minimal further buildup of pressures on the environ-ment caused by agricultural practices.

I conclude by reiterating the importance of developing sustainable local food production and of rural development in the low-income countries. Most of them depend highly on agriculture for employment and income as an important and, often, the critical component of any strategy to improve their levels of food security and alleviate poverty. It is for this reason that sustain-able agricultural and rural development is given enhanced priority in *The Strategic Framework for FAO: 2000–2015*.

Jacques Diouf
Director-General
Food and Agriculture Organization
of the United Nations

Contents

Acknowledgements

This summary document, which is derived from a full technical report under the same title, was prepared mainly by Paul Harrison. The full report is the product of cooperative work by most technical units of FAO. It was prepared by a team led by Jelle Bruinsma under the general direction of Hartwig de Haen, Assistant Director-General, Economic and Social Department. Members of the core team were Nikos Alexandratos, Josef Schmidhuber, Gerold Bödeker and Maria-Grazia Ottaviani.

In addition to the contributions made by the members of the core team, the following FAO staff members and consultants (in alphabetical order) made technical contributions and drafted sections or chapters of the full report: Clare Bishop, Giacomo Branca, Robert Brinkman, Sumiter Broca, Concha Calpe, Lawrence Clarke, Jean-Marc Faurès, Günther Fischer, Theodor Friedrich, René Gommes, Ali Gürkan, David Hallam, Jippe Hoogeveen, Simon Mack, Michael Martin, Jorge Mernies, Rebecca Metzner, Miles Mielke, Nancy Morgan, Freddy Nachtergaele, Loganaden Naiken, CTS Nair, Nquu Nguyen, David Norse, Joachim Otte, Jan Poulisse, Terri Raney, Nadia Scialabba, Kostas Stamoulis, Henning Steinfeld, Peter Thoenes, Vivian Timon, Bruce Traill, Dat Tran, Jeff Tschirley, David Vanzetti, Ulf Wijkstrom and Alberto Zezza. The nature of their contributions is specified in the Acknowledgements of the full report.

Members of the Working Group for the FAO Priority Area for Interdisciplinary Action on Global Perspective Studies provided comments on the various drafts.

Green Ink Ltd, under the direction of Simon Chater, undertook the editing, layout and artwork. FAO's Publishing and Multimedia Service was responsible for the final editing and printing.

About this report

This report is a shorter account of the results of the FAO study, *Agriculture: towards 2015/30*. It presents the latest FAO assessment of long-term developments in world food, nutrition and agriculture, including the forestry and fisheries sectors. It is the product of an interdisciplinary exercise, involving most of FAO's technical units and disciplines, and continues the tradition of FAO's periodical perspective studies for global agriculture, the latest of which was published in 1995 (Alexandratos, 1995). Earlier editions were Alexandratos (1988), FAO (1981) and FAO (1970).

The projections were carried out in considerable detail, covering about 140 countries and 32 crop and livestock commodities (see Annex 1). For nearly all the developing countries, the main factors contributing to the growth of agricultural production were identified and analysed separately. Sources of productivity growth, such as higher crop yields and livestock carcass weights, were distinguished from other growth resources, such as the area of cultivated land and the sizes of livestock herds. Special attention was given to land, which was broken down into five classes for rainfed agriculture and a sixth for irrigated agriculture. This level of detail proved both necessary and advantageous in identifying the main issues likely to emerge for world agriculture over the next 30 years. Specifically, it helped to spot local production and resource constraints, to gauge country-specific requirements for food imports and to assess progress and failure in the fight against hunger and undernourishment. The high degree of detail was also necessary for integrating the expertise of FAO specialists from various disciplines, as the analysis drew heavily on the judgement of in-house experts. Owing to space and other constraints, the results are, however, mainly presented at the aggregate regional and sectoral levels, which can mask diverging developments between individual countries and commodities. Likewise, space considerations militated against the inclusion of references to the numerous sources drawn upon in this report. References have therefore been limited to statistical sources and the sources of figures, tables and maps. These are given on p. 96. A complete list of references is provided in the main technical report.

Another important feature of this report is that its approach is "positive" rather than "normative". This means that its assumptions and projections reflect the most likely future but not necessarily the most desirable one. For example, the report finds that the goal of the 1996 World Food Summit — to halve the number of chronically undernourished people by no later than 2015 — is unlikely to be accomplished, even though this would be highly desirable. Similarly, the report finds that agriculture will probably continue to expand into wetlands and rainforests, even though this is undoubtedly undesirable. In general, the projections presented are therefore not goals of an FAO strategy but rather a basis for action, to cope both with existing problems that are likely to persist and with new ones that may emerge. It should also be stressed that these projections are certainly not trend extrapolations. Instead, they in-corporate a multitude of assumptions about the future and often represent significant deviations from past trends.

A long-term assessment of world food, nutrition and agriculture could deal with a great number of issues, the relevance of which depends on the reader's interest in a particular country, region or topic. As a global study, however, this report had to be selective in the issues it addresses. The main focus is on how the world will feed itself in the future and what the need to produce more food means for its natural resource base. The base year for the study is the three-year average for 1997-99 and projections are made for the years 2015 and 2030. The choice of 2015 allows assessment of whether or not the goal of the 1996 World Food Summit — to halve the number of chronically under-nourished people — is likely to be reached. Extending the horizon to 2030 creates a sufficiently long period for the analysis of issues pertaining to the world's resource base — in other words, the world's ability to cope with further degradation of agricultural land, desertification, deforestation, global warming and water scarcity, as well as increasing demographic pressure. Naturally, the degree of uncertainty increases as the time horizon is extended, so the results envisaged for 2030 should be interpreted more cautiously than those for 2015.

The analysis is, *inter alia*, based on the long-term developments expected by other organizations. The population projections, for instance, reflect the latest assessment (2000 Assessment, Medium Variant) available from the United Nations (UN, 2001), while those for incomes are largely based on the latest projections of gross domestic product (GDP) from the World Bank. Most of the agricultural data are from FAO's database (FAOSTAT), as in July 2001. Because these assumptions critically shape the projected outcomes, it is important to note that they can change significantly, even over the short term. For example, the historical data and the projections for the growth of population and GDP used in the 1995 study have since been revised in many countries, often to a significant extent. World population in the 1995 study, for instance, was projected at 7.2 billion for 2010, whereas the current UN projections peg the figure at 6.8 billion. Similarly, it is now assumed that sub-Saharan Africa's population will reach 780 million by 2010, compared with 915 million in the 1995 study. The GDP projections for sub-Saharan Africa also differ from those assumed in the 1995 study: per capita income growth over the period 1997-99 to 2015 is now projected at 1.8 percent a year, compared with 0.7 percent in the 1995 study (over the period 1988-90 to 2010). Finally, FAO's historical data for food production, demand and per capita consumption were often drastically revised for the entire time series as more up-to-date information became available.

This report begins by presenting the expected developments in world agricultural demand, production and trade (both in total and by major commodity group), and the implications for food security and undernourishment. It continues with a discussion of the main issues raised by these developments. These include the role of agriculture in rural development, poverty alleviation and overall economic growth, and the effects of globalization and freer trade. The report then discusses production and policy issues in the crop, livestock, forestry and fisheries sectors, including natural resource use and agricultural technology issues. It concludes with an assessment of the environmental implications of agricultural production, including its interactions with climate change.

Executive summary

In recent years the growth rates of world agricultural production and crop yields have slowed. This has raised fears that the world may not be able to grow enough food and other commodities to ensure that future populations are adequately fed.

However, the slowdown has occurred not because of shortages of land or water but rather because demand for agricultural products has also slowed. This is mainly because world population growth rates have been declining since the late 1960s, and fairly high levels of food consumption per person are now being reached in many countries, beyond which further rises will be limited. But it is also the case that a stubbornly high share of the world's population remains in absolute poverty and so lacks the necessary income to translate its needs into effective demand.

As a result, the growth in world demand for agricultural products is expected to fall from an average 2.2 percent a year over the past 30 years to 1.5 percent a year for the next 30. In developing countries the slowdown will be more dramatic, from 3.7 percent to 2 percent, partly as a result of China having passed the phase of rapid growth in its demand for food.

This study suggests that world agricultural production can grow in line with demand, provided that the necessary national and international policies to promote agriculture are put in place. Global shortages are unlikely, but serious problems already exist at national and local levels and may worsen unless focused efforts are made.

Food and nutrition

Massive strides have been made in improving food security. The proportion of people living in developing countries with average food intakes below 2 200 kcal per day fell from 57 percent in 1964-66 to just 10 percent in 1997-99. Yet 776 million people in developing countries remain undernourished — about one person in six.

Global progress in nutrition is expected to continue, in parallel with a reduction in poverty as projected by the World Bank. The incidence of undernourishment should fall from 17 percent of the population of developing countries at present to 11 percent in 2015 and just 6 percent in 2030. By 2030, three-quarters of the population of the developing world could be living in countries where less than 5 percent of people are undernourished. Less than 8 percent live in such countries at present.

Despite impressive reductions in the *proportion* of undernourished, continuing population growth means that progress in reducing the total *number* will be slower. The World Food Summit of 1996 set a target of halving the number of undernourished people to about 410 million by 2015. This study's projections suggest that this may be difficult to achieve: some 610 million people could still be undernourished in that year, and even by 2030 about 440 million undernourished may remain. Priority for local food production and reduced inequality of access to food could improve this performance. The problem of undernourishment will tend to become more tractable and easier to address through policy interventions, both national and international, as the number of countries with high incidence declines.

Agriculture, poverty and international trade

Undernourishment is a central manifestation of poverty. It also deepens other aspects of poverty, by reducing the capacity for work and resistance to disease, and by affecting children's mental development and educational achievements.

Currently, one in four people in developing countries are living in extreme poverty, subsisting on less than US$1 a day. This proportion is down from almost one-third in 1990. But because of population growth the fall in numbers has been slower, from 1269 million to 1134 million. The latest World Bank assessment to 2015 suggests that such reductions in global poverty could continue. Sub-Saharan Africa is the exception, however. Here the numbers of poor rose steeply during the 1990s and seem likely to continue to do so. Seven out of ten of the world's poor still live in rural areas. Growth in the agricultural sector has a crucial role to play in improving the incomes of poor people, by providing farm jobs and stimulating off-farm employment. Some direct nutritional interventions may also be needed — such as vitamin and mineral supplementation of basic foods — while health, water and sanitation measures to reduce the effects of illness on food absorption will also be important.

Trade has an important role to play in improving food security and fostering agriculture. Some estimates put the potential annual increase in global welfare from freer trade in agriculture as high as US$165 billion. But the progress made in the current round of trade negotiations has been limited and the benefits so far remain modest. If future reforms focus too narrowly on the removal of subsidies in the countries of the Organisation for Economic Co-operation and Development (OECD), most of the gains will probably be reaped by consumers in developed countries. Developing countries should benefit more from the removal of trade barriers for products in which they have a comparative advantage (such as sugar, fruits and vegetables), from reduced tariffs for processed agricultural commodities, and from deeper preferential access to markets for the least developed countries.

Internal reforms are also needed within developing countries if free trade is to contribute to poverty reduction. Such reforms include: a reduction of the bias against agriculture in national policy making; the opening of borders for long-term foreign investments; the introduction of schemes to improve food quality and safety; investments in roads, irrigation, seeds and skills; improved quality standards; and safety nets for the poor who face higher food prices.

Globalization in food and agriculture holds promise as well as presenting problems. It has generally led to progress in reducing poverty in Asia. But it has also led to the rise of multinational food companies with the potential to disempower farmers in many countries. Developing countries need the legal and administrative frameworks to ward off the threats while reaping the benefits.

Crop production

The annual growth rate of world demand for cereals has declined from 2.5 percent a year in the 1970s and 1.9 percent a year in the 1980s to only 1 percent a year in the 1990s. Annual cereal use per person (including animal feeds) peaked in the mid-1980s at 334 kg and has since fallen to 317 kg.

The decline is not cause for alarm: it was above all the natural result of slower population growth and shifts in human diets and animal feeds. However, in the 1990s it was accentuated by a number of temporary factors, including serious recessions in the transition countries and some East and Southeast Asian countries.

The growth rate of demand for cereals is expected to rise again to 1.4 percent a year to 2015, slowing to 1.2 percent per year thereafter. In developing countries overall, cereal production is not expected to keep pace with demand. The net cereal deficits of these countries, which amounted to 103 million tonnes or 9 percent of consumption in 1997-99, could rise to 265 million tonnes by 2030, when they will be 14 percent of consumption. This gap can be bridged by increased surpluses from traditional grain exporters, and by new exports from the transition countries, which are expected to shift from being net importers to being net exporters.

Oilcrops have seen the fastest increase in area of any crop sector, expanding by 75 million ha from the mid-1970s until the end of the 1990s, while cereal area fell by 28 million ha over the same period. Future per capita consumption of oilcrops is expected to rise more rapidly than that of cereals. These crops will account for 45 out of every 100 extra kilocalories added to average diets in developing countries between now and 2030.

Sources of growth in crop production

There are three main sources of growth in crop production: expanding the land area, increasing the frequency with which it is cropped (often through irrigation), and boosting yields. It has been suggested that we may be approaching the ceiling of what is possible for all three sources.

A detailed examination of production potentials does not support this view at the global level, although in some countries, and even in whole regions, serious problems already exist and could deepen.

Land. Less new agricultural land will be opened up than in the past. In the coming 30 years, developing countries will need an extra 120 million ha for crops, an overall increase of 12.5 percent. This is only half the rate of increase observed between 1961-63 and 1997-99.

At global level there is adequate unused potential farmland. A comparison of soils, terrains and climates with the needs of major crops suggests that an extra 2.8 billion ha are suitable in varying degrees for the rainfed production of arable and permanent crops. This is almost twice as much as is currently farmed. However, only a fraction of this extra land is realistically available for agricultural expansion in the foreseeable future, as much is needed to preserve forest cover and to support infrastructural development. Accessibility and other constraints also stand in the way of any substantial expansion.

More than half the land that could be opened up is in just seven countries of tropical Latin America and sub-Saharan Africa, whereas other regions and countries face a shortage of suitable land. In the Near East and North Africa, 87 percent of suitable land was already being farmed in 1997-99, while in South Asia the figure is no less than 94 percent. In these regions, intensification through improved management and technologies will be the main, indeed virtually the only, source of production growth. In many places land degradation threatens the productivity of existing farmland and pasture.

Water. Irrigation is crucial to the world's food supplies. In 1997-99, irrigated land made up only about one-fifth of the total arable area in developing countries but produced two-fifths of all crops and close to three-fifths of cereal production.

The role of irrigation is expected to increase still further. The developing countries as a whole are likely to expand their irrigated area from 202 million ha in 1997-99 to 242 million ha by 2030. Most of this expansion will occur in land-scarce areas where irrigation is already crucial.

The net increase in irrigated land is predicted to be less than 40 percent of that achieved since the early 1960s. There appears to be enough unused irrigable land to meet future needs: FAO studies suggest a total irrigation potential of some 402 million ha in developing countries, of which only half is currently in use. However, water resources will be a major factor constraining expansion in South Asia, which will be using 41 percent of its renewable freshwater resources by 2030, and in the Near East and North Africa, which will be using 58 percent. These regions will need to achieve greater efficiency in water use.

Yields. In the past four decades, rising yields accounted for about 70 percent of the increase in crop production in the developing countries. The 1990s saw a slowdown in the growth of yields. Wheat yields, for example, grew at an average 3.8 percent a year between 1961 and 1989, but at only 2 percent a year between 1989 and 1999. For rice the respective rates fell by more than half, from 2.3 percent to 1.1 percent.

Yield growth will continue to be the dominant factor underlying increases in crop production in the future. In developing countries, it will account for about 70 percent of growth in crop production to 2030. To meet production projections, future yield growth will not need to be as rapid as in the past. For wheat yields, an annual rise of only 1.2 percent a year is needed over the next 30 years. The picture for other crops is similar. Growth in fertilizer use in developing countries is expected to slow to 1.1 percent per year over the next three decades, a continuation of the slowdown already under way.

Overall, it is estimated that some 80 percent of future increases in crop production in developing countries will have to come from intensification: higher yields, increased multiple cropping and shorter fallow periods.

Improved technology

New technology is needed for areas with shortages of land or water, or with particular problems of soil or climate. These are frequently areas with a high concentration of poor people, where such technology could play a key role in improving food security.

Agricultural production could probably meet expected demand over the period to 2030 even without major advances in modern biotechnology. However, the new techniques of molecular analysis could give a welcome boost to productivity, particularly in areas with special difficulties, thereby improving the incomes of the poor, just as the green revolution did in large parts of Asia during the 1960s to 1980s.

Needed for the twenty-first century is a second, doubly green revolution in agricultural technology. Productivity increases are still vital, but must be combined with environmental protection or restoration, while new technologies must be both affordable by, and geared to the needs of, the poor and undernourished.

Biotechnology offers promise as a means of improving food security and reducing pressures on the environment, provided the perceived environmental threats from biotechnology itself are addressed. Genetically modified crop varieties — resistant to drought, waterlogging, soil acidity, salinity and extreme temperatures — could help to sustain farming in marginal areas and to restore degraded lands to production. Pest-resistant varieties can reduce the need for pesticides.

However, the widespread use of genetically modified varieties will depend on whether or not food safety and environmental concerns can be adequately addressed. Indeed, the spread of these varieties, in the developed countries at least, has recently slowed somewhat in response to these concerns, which must be addressed through improved testing and safety protocols if progress is to resume.

Meanwhile, other promising technologies have emerged that combine increased production with improved environmental protection. These include no-till or conservation agriculture, and the lower-input approaches of integrated pest or nutrient management and organic agriculture.

Livestock

Diets in developing countries are changing as incomes rise. The share of staples, such as cereals, roots and tubers, is declining, while that of meat, dairy products and oilcrops is rising.

Between 1964-66 and 1997-99, per capita meat consumption in developing countries rose by 150 percent, and that of milk and dairy products by 60 percent. By 2030, per capita consumption of livestock products could rise by a further 44 percent. As in the past, poultry consumption will grow fastest.

Productivity improvements are likely to be a major source of growth. Milk yields should improve, while breeding and improved management will increase average carcass weights and offtake rates. This will allow increased production with lower growth in animal numbers, and a corresponding slowdown in the growth of environmental damage from grazing or wastes.

In developing countries, demand will grow faster than production, producing a growing trade deficit. In meat products this will rise steeply, from 1.2 million tonnes a year in 1997-99 to 5.9 million tonnes in 2030 (despite growing meat exports from Latin America), while in milk and dairy products the rise will be less steep but still considerable, from 20 million to 39 million tonnes a year.

An increasing share of livestock production will probably come from industrial enterprises. In recent years production from this sector has grown twice as fast as that from more traditional mixed farming systems and more than six times faster than from grazing systems.

Forestry
During the 1990s the world's total forest area shrank by 9.4 million ha — about three times the size of Belgium — each year. However, the rate of deforestation was slower in the 1990s than in the 1980s. Industrial and transition countries expanded their forest areas, and many developing countries — including Bangladesh, China, India, Turkey and Viet Nam — are now planting more forest area than they cut.

The crop projections suggest that cropland will need to expand by an extra 120 million ha by 2030, while urban land areas will continue to grow by a considerable amount. Much of this extra land will have to come from forest clearance. In addition, by 2030 annual world consumption of industrial roundwood is expected to rise by 60 percent over current levels, to around 2 400 million m³.

Even so, deforestation is expected to slow further in the coming decades and the world is unlikely to face a wood supply crisis. Production of wood-based materials is continually increasing in efficiency. The area of plantations is also growing rapidly: production of industrial roundwood from plantations is expected to double by 2030, from 400 million m³ today, to around 800 million m³. In addition, a big increase in tree-growing outside forests and plantations — along roads, in towns, around homes and on farms — will boost the supply of wood and other tree products.

The central challenges for the forestry sector are to find ways of managing natural and cultivated tree resources so as to increase production, improve the food security and energy supply of the poor, and safeguard the environmental services and biodiversity provided by forests.

Fisheries
World fisheries production has kept ahead of population growth over the past three decades. Total fish production almost doubled, from 65 million tonnes in 1970 to 125 million tonnes in 1999, when world average intake of fish, crustaceans and molluscs reached 16.3 kg per person. By 2030, annual fish

consumption is likely to rise to some 150 to160 million tonnes, or between 19 and 20 kg per person.

This amount is significantly lower than the potential demand, because environmental factors are expected to limit supply. By the turn of the century, three-quarters of ocean fish stocks were overfished, depleted or exploited up to their maximum sustainable yield. Further growth in the marine catch can be only modest. During the 1990s the marine catch levelled out at 80 to 85 million tonnes a year, not far from its maximum sustainable yield.

Aquaculture compensated for this marine slowdown, doubling its share of world fish production during the 1990s. It will continue to grow rapidly, at rates of 5 to 7 percent a year up to 2015. In all sectors of fishing it will be essential to pursue forms of management conducive to sustainable exploitation, especially for resources under common ownership or no ownership.

Environment and climate

Over the next 30 years, many of the environmental problems associated with agriculture will remain serious. Loss of biodiversity caused by the expansion and intensification of production often continues unabated even in the developed countries, where nature is highly valued and, supposedly, protected.

Nitrogen fertilizers are a major source of water and air pollution. The crop projections imply slower growth in the use of these fertilizers than in the past, but the increase could still be significant for pollution. Projections also suggest a 60 percent increase in emissions of ammonia and methane from the livestock sector. Comprehensive measures will be needed to control and reduce air and water pollution from these sources.

Global warming is not expected to depress food availability at the global level, but at the regional and local levels there may be significant impacts. Current projections suggest that the potential for crop production will increase in temperate and northerly latitudes, while in parts of the tropics and subtropics it may decline. This may further deepen the dependence of developing countries on food imports, though at the same time it may improve the ability of temperate exporters to fill the gap. Rising sea levels will threaten crop production and livelihoods in countries with large areas of low-lying land, such as Bangladesh and Egypt.

Food insecurity for some vulnerable rural groups in developing countries may well worsen. By 2030, climate change is projected to depress cereal production in Africa by 2 to 3 percent. Improved seeds and increased fertilizer use should more than compensate, but this factor will still weigh heavily on efforts to make progress.

Forestry and agriculture both contribute to human impact on climate. The burning of biomass — in deforestation, savannah fires, the disposal of crop residues and cooking with firewood or dung — is a major source of atmospheric carbon dioxide, while fertilizers and animal wastes create large emissions of nitrous oxide and ammonia.

Forestry can help to soak up some of the carbon released by human activities. Between 1995 and 2050, slower deforestation, together with regeneration and plantation development, could reduce carbon dioxide emissions by the equivalent of 12 to 15 percent of all fossil fuel emissions.

Farming also has a positive role to play. By 2030 the amount of carbon locked up in cropland soils, as soil organic matter from crop residues and manure, could rise by 50 percent if better management practices are introduced.

The projections at a glance

Population (millions)	1979-81	1997-99	2015	2030	2050
World	4 430	5 900	7 207	8 270	9 322
Developing countries	3 259	4 595	5 858	6 910	7 987
Industrial countries	789	892	951	979	986
Transition countries	382	413	398	381	349

Population growth (% per annum)	1979 to 1999	1989 to 1999	1997-99 to 2015	2015 to 2030	2030 to 2050
World	1.6	1.5	1.2	0.9	0.6
Developing countries	1.9	1.7	1.4	1.1	0.7
Industrial countries	0.7	0.7	0.4	0.2	0.0
Transition countries	0.5	0.1	- 0.2	- 0.3	- 0.4

GDP growth (% per annum)	1997-99 to 2015 total	2015 to 2030 total	1997-99 to 2015 per capita	2015 to 2030 per capita
World	3.5	3.8	2.3	2.9
Developing countries	5.1	5.5	3.7	4.4
Industrial countries	3.0	3.0	2.6	2.8
Transition countries	3.7	4.0	4.0	4.3

Growth in demand for agricultural products (% per annum)	1969 to 1999	1979 to 1999	1989 to 1999	1997-99 to 2015	2015 to 2030
World	2.2	2.1	2.0	1.6	1.4
Developing countries	3.7	3.7	4.0	2.2	1.7
Industrial countries	1.1	1.0	1.0	0.7	0.6
Transition countries	- 0.2	- 1.7	- 4.4	0.5	0.4

Growth in agricultural production (% per annum)	1969 to 1999	1979 to 1999	1989 to 1999	1997-99 to 2015	2015 to 2030
World	2.2	2.1	2.0	1.6	1.3
Developing countries	3.5	3.7	3.9	2.0	1.7
Industrial countries	1.3	1.0	1.4	0.8	0.6
Transition countries	- 0.4	- 1.7	- 4.7	0.6	0.6

Calorie consumption (kcal/capita/day)	1961-63	1979-81	1997-99	2015	2030
World	2 283	2 552	2 803	2 940	3 050
Developing countries	1 960	2 312	2 681	2 850	2 980
Industrial countries	2 891	3 135	3 380	3 440	3 500
Transition countries	3 154	3 389	2 906	3 060	3 180

Undernourishment	Million people				% of population			
	1990-92	1997-99	2015	2030	1990-92	1997-99	2015	2030
World		815				14		
Developing countries	816	777	610	443	20	17	11	6
Industrial countries		11				1		
Transition countries		27				6		

Cereals	Million tonnes				% per annum			
	1979-81	1997-99	2015	2030	1979 to 1999	1989 to 1999	1997-99 to 2015	2015 to 2030
World								
Production	1 442	1 889	2 387	2 838	1.4	1.0	1.4	1.2
Food	706	1 003	1 227	1 406	1.9	1.4	1.2	0.9
Feed	575	657	911	1 148	0.6	0.6	1.9	1.5
Developing countries								
Production	649	1 026	1 354	1 652	2.5	2.1	1.6	1.3
Food	524	790	1 007	1 185	2.2	1.7	1.4	1.1
Feed	113	222	397	573	3.8	4.4	3.5	2.5
Net trade	- 66	- 103	- 190	- 265				

Meat	Million tonnes				% per annum			
	1979-81	1997-99	2015	2030	1979 to 1999	1989 to 1999	1997-99 to 2015	2015 to 2030
World								
Production	132	218	300	376	2.8	2.7	1.9	1.5
Food	130	214	297	373	2.8	2.7	1.9	1.5
Developing countries								
Production	45	116	181	247	5.5	5.9	2.7	2.1
Food	44	116	184	252	5.6	6.1	2.7	2.1
Net trade	- 0.2	- 1.2	- 3.9	- 5.9				

Vegetable oils and oilseeds (oil equivalent)	Million tonnes				% per annum			
	1979-81	1997-99	2015	2030	1979 to 1999	1989 to 1999	1997-99 to 2015	2015 to 2030
World								
Production	50	104	157	217	4.1	4.3	2.5	2.2
Food	37	67	98	130	3.3	2.8	2.3	1.9
Industrial use	8	23	45	71	6.1	6.9	3.9	3.1
Developing countries								
Production	29	68	109	156	5.0	4.7	2.8	2.4
Food	21	45	73	102	4.3	3.6	2.9	2.2
Industrial use	3	13	26	41	8.2	10.2	4.4	3.1
Net trade	1.5	4.0	3.4	3.5				

Arable land (million ha)	Total			Irrigated			
	1997-99	2015	2030	1979-81	1997-99	2015	2030
World	1 608			210	271		
Developing countries	956	1017	1076	151	202	221	242
Industrial countries	387			37	42		
Transition countries	265			22	25		

Crop land and yields in developing countries	Harvested land (million ha)				Yield (tonnes/ha)			
	1979-81	1997-99	2015	2030	1979-81	1997-99	2015	2030
Wheat	96	111	113	118	1.6	2.5	3.1	3.5
Rice (paddy)	138	157	162	164	2.7	3.6	4.2	4.7
Maize	76	97	118	136	2.0	2.8	3.4	4.0
All cereals	408	465	497	528	1.9	2.6	3.2	3.6
% of total	60	55	53	51				

Long-term Perspectives

The outlook for agriculture

The rate of growth in world demand for agricultural products has slowed, because population growth has declined and fairly high levels of food consumption have been reached in many countries. Growth in demand will slow still further in the future. The world as a whole has the production potential to cope with demand. However, developing countries will become more dependent on agricultural imports, and food security in many poor areas will not improve without substantial increases in local production.

So far, world agriculture has been able to respond to the rising demand for crop and livestock products. Although the world's population doubled between 1960 and 2000 and levels of nutrition improved markedly, the prices of rice, wheat and maize — the world's major food staples — fell by around 60 percent. The fall in prices indicates that, globally, supplies not only kept pace with demand, but even outstripped it.

Although global demand for agricultural products has continued to rise, it has done so less rapidly in recent decades. Between 1969 and 1989 demand grew at an average of 2.4 percent a year, but this fell to only 2 percent in the decade from 1989.

Apart from temporary factors (foremost among them a decline in consumption in the transition economies in the 1990s), there were two more enduring reasons for the slowdown:
- The growth rate of world population peaked in the late 1960s at 2 percent a year and slowed thereafter.
- A rising proportion of the world's population had reached fairly high levels of food consumption, so the scope for further increase was limited. By 1997-99, 61 percent of the world's population were living in countries where average food consumption per person was above 2 700 kcal per day.

Demand for agricultural products will continue to grow more slowly

These factors will continue to influence trends in demand over the next three decades. For example, world population will go on rising, but less rapidly, growing at an average of 1.1 percent a year up to 2030, compared with 1.7 percent a year over the past 30 years.

As a result, future demand for agricultural products is expected to slow further — to 1.6 percent a year for the period 1997-99 to 2015 and to 1.4 percent for 2015 to 2030. In developing countries the slowdown will be more dramatic, from 3.7 percent for the past 30 years to an average 2 percent for the next 30.

The forces underlying this slowdown can be seen in the example of China, which has been one of the major engines of growth in the demand for food and agricultural products in the world and in the developing countries over the past few decades. By 1997-99 the Chinese

By 1997-99, 61 percent of the world's population were living in countries where average food consumption per person was above 2 700 kcal per day.

had reached an average daily food consumption of 3 040 kcal — only 10 percent short of the level in industrial countries. Over the next three decades the country's aggregate food consumption is expected to grow at only a quarter of the rate seen in the past three decades, while its population will grow at a third of its past rate. Given the sheer size of China's population, these shifts alone will have a huge effect on the global situation. Many other countries, including some of the largest ones, will be undergoing very similar shifts that will further lower the growth of demand.

India's daily average food energy intake per person is still below 2 500 kcal, a level at which there is considerable scope for further increases, while her population will be growing at an average of over 1 percent a year over the next 30 years. Could India take over China's role as a major engine of growth in world agricultural demand? This is not expected, because India's cultural traditions favour vegetarianism, which will hold back the country's demand for meat and animal feeds at rates well below those seen in China.

Agricultural trade deficits of developing countries will worsen

Traditionally, the developing countries as a whole have had a net surplus in agricultural trade. In value terms this peaked at US$17.5 billion in 1977. The trend since then has been for their imports to grow faster than their exports. The agricultural trade balance of the developing countries has gradually dwindled until, by the mid-1990s, it was more often negative than positive. The highest recorded deficit was US$6 billion, in 1996.

This overall trend masks a complex picture which varies from one commodity to another and from one country to another. The drastic decline in developing countries' net surplus in sugar, oilseeds and vegetable oils, for example, reflects growing consumption and imports in several developing countries and the effects of protectionist policies in the major industrial countries. For commodities produced almost entirely in developing countries and consumed predominantly in the industrial countries, such as coffee and cocoa, slow growth in demand prevented the trade balance of the developing

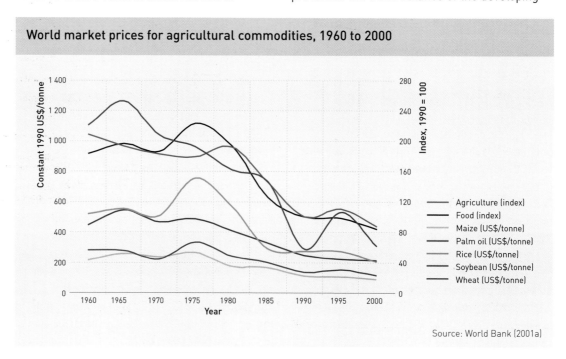

World market prices for agricultural commodities, 1960 to 2000

Source: World Bank (2001a)

countries from improving. Fluctuating and, on balance, declining prices further contributed to the problem.

The projections to 2030 show the agricultural trade deficit of developing countries growing still further. In particular, net imports of cereals and livestock products will continue to rise quite rapidly.

Production will keep pace with demand, but food insecurity will persist

Detailed analysis shows that, globally, there is enough land, soil and water, and enough

potential for further growth in yields, to make the necessary production feasible. Yield growth will be slower than in the past, but at the global level this is not necessarily cause for alarm because slower growth in production is needed in the future than in the past. However, the feasible can only become the actual if the policy environment is favourable towards agriculture.

Globally, producers have satisfied effective market demand in the past, and there is every likelihood that they will continue to do so. But effective demand does not represent the total need for food and other agricultural products,

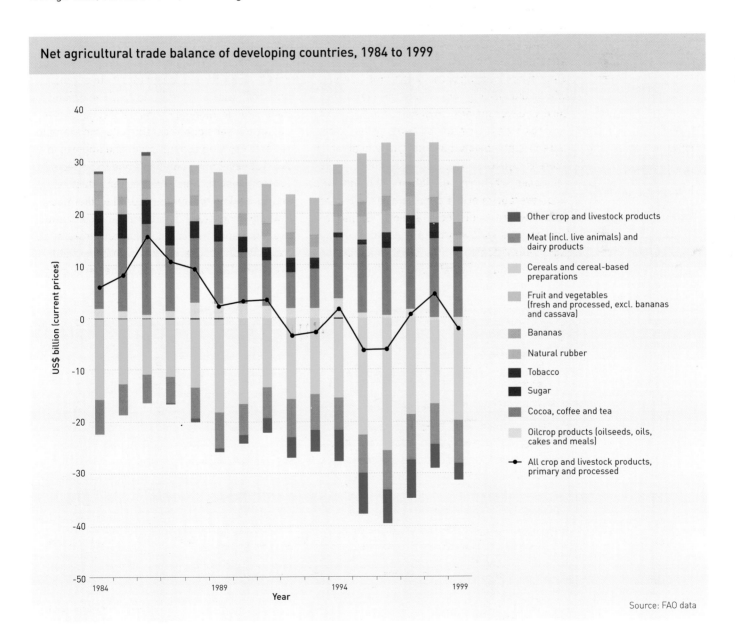

Net agricultural trade balance of developing countries, 1984 to 1999

US$ billion (current prices)

Legend:
- Other crop and livestock products
- Meat (incl. live animals) and dairy products
- Cereals and cereal-based preparations
- Fruit and vegetables (fresh and processed, excl. bananas and cassava)
- Bananas
- Natural rubber
- Tobacco
- Sugar
- Cocoa, coffee and tea
- Oilcrop products (oilseeds, oils, cakes and meals)
- All crop and livestock products, primary and processed

Year

Source: FAO data

because hundreds of millions of people lack the money to buy what they need or the resources to produce it themselves.

Thus, even if there is sufficient potential for production in the world as a whole, there will still be problems of food security at the household or national level. In urban areas, food insecurity usually reflects low incomes, but in poor rural areas it is often inseparable from problems affecting food production. In many areas of the developing world, the majority of people still depend on local agriculture for food and/or livelihoods but the potential of local resources to support further increases in production is very limited, at least under existing technological conditions. Examples are semi-arid areas and areas with problem soils.

In such areas agriculture must be developed through support for agricultural research and extension and the provision of credit and infrastructure, while other income-earning opportunities are created. If this is not done, local food insecurity will remain widespread, even in the midst of global plenty.

Prospects for food and nutrition

Global progress in improving human nutrition will continue, but in numerical terms it will be slow. Even by 2030, hundreds of millions of poor people will remain under-nourished unless local food production is given higher priority and inequality of access to food is reduced. However, the lower incidence of undernourishment will make the problem more tractable through national and international policy interventions.

Progress in improving nutrition has been significant

Freedom from hunger is not only a basic human right: it is essential for the full enjoyment of other rights, such as health, education and work, and everything that flows from these.

The world has made significant progress in raising nutrition levels over the past three decades. These levels are most commonly measured in terms of kilocalories per person per day. People in developing countries need between 1 720 and 1 960 kcal per day for basal metabolism and light activity.

World average food consumption per person has risen by almost a fifth, from 2 360 kcal per person per day in the mid-1960s to 2 800 kcal per person per day today. The gains in the world average reflect predominantly those of the developing countries, given that the industrial and transition economies had fairly high levels of food consumption already in the mid-1960s. Over the period to 1997-99, average daily per capita food consumption in developing countries rose from 2 050 kcal to 2 680 kcal (see Annex Table A3).

The proportion of the world's population living in countries with low average food energy intakes has declined dramatically. In the mid-1960s, no less than 57 percent were living in countries with average intakes below 2 200 kcal per day. India and China both came into this category. By 1997-99, although world population had almost doubled to nearly six billion, this proportion had fallen to just 10 percent. Even the absolute numbers — which decline more slowly because of population growth — fell by over two-thirds, from 1 890 million to 570 million.

At the other extreme, the share of the world's population living in countries with average food energy intakes above 2 700 kcal per person per day has more than doubled, from 30 percent to 61 percent. Rapid gains in some of the largest developing countries, including

China, Brazil, Indonesia and Nigeria, account for much of this progress. India, however, has yet to move into this category.

Over this same period, world annual consumption of cereals for both food and feed has doubled to 1.9 billion tonnes, while that of meat has more than doubled — no mean achievement considering popular fears that the world was running out of potential to increase production. The main forces driving this achievement have included higher incomes, which have increased effective demand, increased supplies, owing to improvements in productivity, and the growth of trade and transport links, which have allowed food deficits in some areas to be covered by surpluses from other areas.

Yet hundreds of millions remain undernourished

This remarkable achievement has nevertheless left out a massive number of people, who continue to fare badly. In 1997-99 there were still 777 million undernourished people in developing countries — about one person in six. This represents only a modest decline from the figure of 816 million for 1990-92.

In China, huge reductions in poverty raised national average food consumption substantially — and this had a strong effect on the global picture. If China is removed from the picture, it becomes clear that the number of undernourished people actually increased in the other developing countries, by almost 40 million.

> In 1997-99 there were still 777 million undernourished people in developing countries — about one person in six.

The region with the largest number of undernourished people in 1997-99 was South Asia, where 303 million or just under a quarter of the population remained undernourished. The region with the highest proportion was sub-Saharan Africa, where over a third of the total population, or 194 million people, were undernourished.

In 1997-99, some 30 developing countries still had average per capita food consumption of below 2 200 kcal per day. War and civil strife were significant factors in no less than half of these countries. In most of them, food consumption today stands at levels below those attained in the past. Some 23 of the 30 are in sub-Saharan Africa, while only 7 are in other regions.

Populations and incomes will continue to grow

Future food consumption patterns are determined by growth in population and in incomes, and by changes in dietary preferences.

The latest projections by the United Nations (UN) show a continuing slowdown in the growth of the world's population. In the medium UN projection, the 6.1 billion people of 2000 will grow to 7.2 billion in 2015 and 8.3 billion in 2030, heading towards 9.3 billion in 2050.

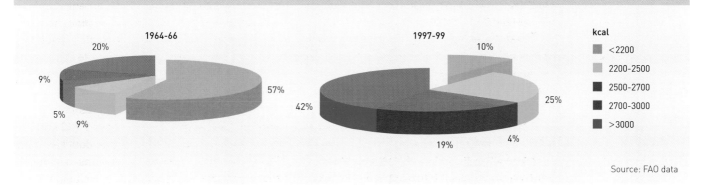

Global progress in nutrition: energy intake levels by percentage of the world's population, 1964-66 and 1997-99

1964-66: 20%, 9%, 5%, 9%, 57%

1997-99: 10%, 25%, 4%, 19%, 42%

kcal
- <2200
- 2200-2500
- 2500-2700
- 2700-3000
- >3000

Source: FAO data

15

Perceptions of a continuing population explosion are false. In fact it is more than 30 years since the world passed its peak population growth rate, of 2.04 percent a year, in the late 1960s. Since then the growth rate has fallen to 1.35 percent. This is expected to fall further to 1.1 percent in the period 2010 to 2015 and to 0.8 percent in 2025 to 2030. There will be a corresponding slowdown in the growth of demand for food.

The absolute numbers added each year are also past their peak of 86 million a year, reached in the late 1980s. Even so, current annual additions of around 77 million still amount to almost a new Germany each year. The yearly increments will taper off only slowly during the study period: even by the period 2025 to 2030 they will still be running at 67 million a year. It is only by the middle of the century that these increments will have fallen significantly, to 43 million per year in 2045 to 2050. Almost all of these increases will be in the developing countries.

By 2030 there will be substantial differences in population growth rates among the developing countries. While East Asia's population will be growing at only 0.4 percent a year, that of sub-Saharan Africa will still be growing at 2.1 percent. By 2030, every third person added to the world's population will be a sub-Saharan African. By 2050, this will rise to every second person.

The second major factor determining the demand for food is growth in incomes. The latest World Bank assessment of future economic growth is less optimistic than its predecessors, but it still projects a rise of 1.9 percent a year in per capita incomes between 2000 and 2015, higher than the 1.2 percent seen in the 1990s.

What will happen to the incidence of poverty under this overall economic scenario is of great importance to food security because poverty and hunger are closely associated. The World Bank has estimated the implications of its economic growth projections for poverty reduction by the year 2015. They are that:
- It is possible to achieve the goal of halving the *proportion* of people living in absolute poverty — defined as an income below US$1 per day — by 2015, over the 1990 level.
- However, it is unlikely that the *number* of poor people can also be halved. This will decline from 1.27 billion in 1990 to 0.75 billion in 2015.
- Much of the decline will be due to development in East and South Asia. Indeed, about half of the decline of 400 million projected for East Asia has already occurred.
- Only in sub-Saharan Africa, where incomes are expected to grow very slowly, are the numbers living in poverty expected to rise, from 240 million in 1990 to 345 million in 2015. By then, two out of five people in the region will be living in poverty.

Average nutrition will improve, but undernourishment will fall only slowly

In the light of these changes in population and incomes, progress in improving nutrition is expected to continue, though more slowly than in the past. Average per capita food consumption in developing countries is projected to rise by 6.3 percent, from 2 680 kcal in 1997-99 to 2 850 kcal in 2015. This is a third of the rise achieved between 1974-76 and 1997-99.

The slowdown is occurring not because of production limits but because many countries have now reached medium to high levels of consumption, beyond which there is less scope than in the past for further increases. Huge countries such as China, where per capita consumption rose from 2 050 kcal per day in the mid-1970s to over 3 000 kcal per day today, have already passed the phase of rapid growth. More and more countries will be attaining such levels over the projection period.

By 2030, three-quarters of the population of the developing world could be living in countries where less than 5 percent of people are undernourished. Only 1 in 13 live in such countries at present.

The World Food Summit of 1996 set a target of halving the numbers of undernourished in developing countries by 2015, compared with the base period of 1990-92. FAO's study has found that the proportion of undernourished people should fall significantly, from 20 percent in 1990-92 to 11 percent by 2015 and 6 percent by 2030. However, in numerical terms the World Food Summit target is unlikely to be met. The total number of undernourished people will probably fall from 815 million in 1990-92 to some 610 million by 2015. Not until 2030 will the numbers fall to 440 million, thereby approaching the 2015 target.

The proportion of the world's population living in countries with per capita food consumption under 2 200 kcal per day will fall to only 2.4 percent in 2030. The reduction in the number of undernourished people will be impressive in some regions: in South Asia, for example, it could fall from 303 million in 1997-99 to 119 million in 2030, while in East Asia the number could halve from its current level of 193 million.

In contrast, in sub-Saharan Africa and the Near East and North Africa, there is likely to be little or no decline in the numbers of undernourished people, although the proportion will approximately halve. By 2030, all regions except sub-Saharan Africa should see the incidence of undernourishment decline to between 4 and 6 percent, down from the range of 9 to 24 percent today. In sub-Saharan Africa, 15 percent of the population or 183 million people will still be undernourished by 2030. This will be by far the highest total for any region, and is only 11 million less than in 1997-99. The fate of sub-Saharan Africa is therefore cause for serious concern.

As incomes rise, access to food should become more equal. This is because poor people spend a high proportion of increases in their incomes on food, whereas there is an upper limit to the amount of food that rich people want to eat. This greater equality will have a significant effect on the numbers of undernourished people. For example, in the 44 countries that will have average per capita food intakes of over 2 700 kcal per day in 2015,

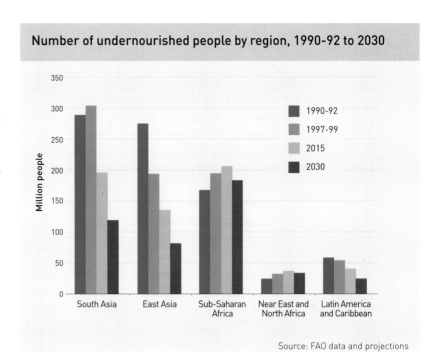

Number of undernourished people by region, 1990-92 to 2030

Legend:
- 1990-92
- 1997-99
- 2015
- 2030

Y-axis: Million people

X-axis categories: South Asia, East Asia, Sub-Saharan Africa, Near East and North Africa, Latin America and Caribbean

Source: FAO data and projections

the number of undernourished people is expected to be 295 million. But if inequality of access to food were to remain unchanged at today's level, this number would be 400 million.

The decline in the numbers of undernourished between now and 2030 will be slow, for several reasons:

- Rapid population growth means that, although the proportion of undernourished may fall, the absolute number will fall much less and may in a few cases even rise. This is an important factor in sub-Saharan Africa and the Near East and North Africa.
- Economic growth will not be fast enough. In the Niger, for example, 3.3 million people or 41 percent of the population were undernourished in 1990-92. To achieve the World Food Summit target, the number of undernourished will need to fall to 1.65 million or 9 percent of the population by 2015. To bring this about would require growth rates far above what the Niger has seen over the past two decades.
- Several countries start from highly adverse conditions, namely low national average food

consumption, high incidence of undernourishment and high projected population growth. For example, nine developing countries had proportions of undernourishment in 1990-92 of over 50 percent (Afghanistan, Angola, Burundi, Democratic Republic of Congo, Eritrea, Ethiopia, Haiti, Mozambique and Somalia). In these countries the proportion of undernourished is expected to fall to 39 percent by 2015 and to 25 percent by 2030. However, because of the relatively high growth rate of this group's population, the absolute numbers affected will rise to 115 million in 2015 and may still be 106 million in 2030. Even these figures are based on projections for growth in food consumption that are much faster than the fastest seen in any comparable period in the past.

• In countries where average food intake is currently low and the majority of people are hungry, reducing inequality of access to food has only a small impact on levels of undernourishment. This is because few people are on diets that are more than barely adequate, so redistributing their food "surplus" does not greatly improve matters. By 2015 there will still be 41 countries with average food intakes of 2 500 kcal per day or less.

• In the future the threshold for defining undernourishment will rise, as ageing reduces the proportion of children in the population. Since children's food energy requirements are lower than those of adults, the average calorie requirement in developing countries will rise by around 3 percent by 2030. If it were not for this rise in the threshold, the number of undernourished estimated for 2030 would be 370 million instead of 440 million.

The number of undernourished can be reduced more rapidly by affording increased priority to agriculture, increasing national food production and reducing inequality of access to food. These three measures should be combined with continuing interventions to cope with the consequences of local food crises, until the root causes of undernourishment have been removed.

It is possible for countries to raise nutrition levels even in the absence of significant economic growth. Mali raised average food consumption by almost a third in the 1980s, although per capita household expenditure fell over this period. Other countries, such as Benin, Burkina Faso, Ghana, Mauritania and Nigeria, achieved similar quantum leaps at times of slow income growth. The common characteristic seems to have been rapid growth in the production of food staples (cereals, roots and tubers), leading to improved self-sufficiency, at least in cereals. Because most agriculture was at or below the subsistence level, increased production led directly to improved food consumption in rural populations.

The problem of undernourishment should become more tractable
The projections imply that the problem of undernourishment should become more tractable in future. This will work in two major ways:

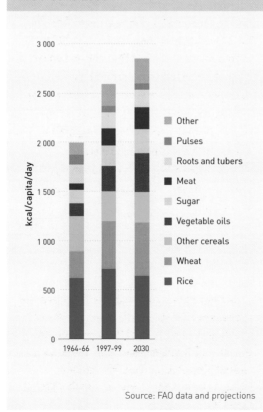

Dietary changes in developing countries, 1964-66 to 2030

kcal/capita/day

Other
Pulses
Roots and tubers
Meat
Sugar
Vegetable oils
Other cereals
Wheat
Rice

1964-66   1997-99   2030

Source: FAO data and projections

How diets will change

Just as world average calorie intakes have increased, so also people's diets have changed. Patterns of food consumption are becoming more similar throughout the world, incorporating higher-quality and more expensive foods such as meat and dairy products.

This trend is partly due to simple preferences. Partly, too, it is due to increased international trade in foods, to the global spread of fast food chains, and to exposure to North American and European dietary habits. Convenience also plays a part, for example the portability and ease of preparation of ready-made bread or pizza, versus root vegetables. Changes in diet closely follow rises in incomes and occur almost irrespective of geography, history, culture or religion. However, cultural and religious factors do explain differences between countries with similar income levels. For example, Hindus abstain from beef or meat in general, Moslems and Jews from pork. Despite similar income levels, Japanese people consume far fewer calories from non-starchy foods than do Americans, as do Thais compared with Brazilians.

Dietary convergence is quite high among the high-income countries of the Organisation for Economic Co-operation and Development (OECD), where food consumption patterns show a 75 percent overlap with those in the United States, meaning that 75 percent of processed food products are based on the same raw materials. Even Japan has been moving closer to other OECD countries, with the overlap rising from 45 percent in 1961 to about 70 percent in 1999. Convergence towards North American dietary patterns is also occurring in other groups of developing countries, though only slowly in some cases, especially in land-locked or politically isolated countries where international influences permeate less easily. However, cultural factors appear to limit convergence to an upper ceiling of around 80 percent, at least for the time being.

These changes in diet have had an impact on the global demand for agricultural products and will go on doing so. Meat consumption in developing countries, for example, has risen from only 10 kg per person per year in 1964-66 to 26 in 1997-99. It is projected to rise still further, to 37 kg per person per year in 2030. Milk and dairy products have also seen rapid growth, from 28 kg per person per year in 1964-66 to 45 kg now, and could rise to 66 kg by 2030. The intake of calories derived from sugar and vegetable oils is expected to increase. However, average human consumption of cereals, pulses, roots and tubers is expected to level off.

- As the incidence of undernourishment diminishes, more and more countries will find it easier to address the problem through national policy interventions. By 2030, three-quarters of the population of developing countries could be living in countries where less than 5 percent of people are undernourished, compared with 7.7 percent at present. This dramatic change will occur because the majority of the most populous countries (Brazil, China, India, Indonesia, Islamic Republic of Iran, Mexico and Pakistan) will shift to the "under-5-percent" category.

- The number of countries with severe problems of undernourishment will become smaller over time. International policy responses will tend to become more feasible and effective, as the total effort need not be spread so thinly. For example, if the projections come true, the number of countries with undernourishment of over 25 percent will fall from 35 at present (accounting for 13 percent of the population of the developing countries) to 15 in 2030 (accounting for only 3.5 percent).

Food and Agriculture in National and International Settings

Poverty and agriculture

Except in most of sub-Saharan Africa, developing countries are making progress towards the UN goal of halving the incidence of poverty by 2015. Growth in agriculture and in non-farm rural activities, as well as improvements in nutrition, will be central to continuing success. Sub-Saharan Africa's continuing descent into poverty is cause for serious concern.

Undernourishment is not merely a symptom of poverty but also one of its causes. Poverty is not simply a lack of income or consumption but includes deprivation in health, education, nutrition, safety, legal and political rights, and many other areas. All these dimensions of deprivation interact with and reinforce each other.

Over the past decade, poverty and the related issue of inequality have moved to the top of the international development agenda. At various summits from the early 1990s onwards, world leaders have proclaimed their commitment to poverty reduction and adopted a series of related targets. These cover a wide range, from infant and child mortality to school enrolment, from gender equality to maternal mortality, from access to health and reproductive health services to the adoption of national strategies for sustainable development. The UN Millennium Declaration, adopted in September 2000, consolidated most of these targets, including that of halving the proportion of people living in extreme poverty by 2015. The international targets, and the indicators used to assess progress towards them, should be viewed neither as finely tuned criteria to guide policy and spending priorities nor as accurate measures of progress. In many poor countries the necessary data are not reliable and may not even be up-to-date. Nor are they necessarily comparable between different countries. But the targets are useful in drawing attention to persistent poverty, and in influencing opinion and creating a sense of urgency among the public, politicians and the development community. The indicators can also serve as rough guides to assess whether progress is being made.

Overall progress and prospects

At the beginning of the twenty-first century, over 1.1 billion people are living in extreme poverty, subsisting on less than US$1 a day. Significant, but uneven, progress is being made towards meeting the 2015 target of halving the proportion of people living in poverty in developing countries. This proportion fell from 32 percent in 1990 to 25 percent in 1999. However, because of population growth, the reduction in numbers was less dramatic, from 1 269 million to 1 134 million.

The regional picture was highly diverse. In East Asia, poverty fell very steeply during the 1990s. In South Asia, although the proportion of poor fell, the total number remained almost constant. In sub-Saharan Africa, the proportion remained virtually unchanged, while the number rose steeply.

The latest World Bank projections suggest that the target of halving the *proportion* of people living in poverty in the developing countries by 2015 can be achieved. However, even if this target were met, because of population growth the result would be a fall of less than 30 percent in the absolute *number* of poor. In sub-Saharan Africa the target seems unattainable: projections suggest only a small reduction in the proportion and a continued rise in the number living in poverty.

Even the World Bank projections assume faster economic growth rates than in the past. The Bank stresses that, if the slow growth of the 1990s persists, then the number of people living in extreme poverty will remain near current levels for the next 15 years.

Faster growth of incomes is essential for poverty reduction everywhere. Reducing inequality is equally crucial, especially in countries where this is pronounced. According to some estimates, countries where inequality is high will need twice as much growth as those where it is low to meet the poverty target.

Why better nutrition has to come first

Food and agriculture are centrally involved in both the generation and the reduction of poverty.

Undernourishment is a characteristic feature of poverty and a direct violation of a universally recognized human right. It also deepens other aspects of poverty, in the following important ways:
- It leaves people more susceptible to illness. Episodes of illness in turn reduce the intake and absorption of food, producing a vicious downward spiral in which hunger and disease feed off each other.
- When pregnant and nursing mothers are undernourished, babies are born underweight and start life with a nutritional handicap that can affect their health throughout their lives.
- Undernourishment can affect brain development in the womb and attentiveness in class, and so is associated with poor educational performance.
- When energy and protein intakes are inadequate for the requirements of work, muscle mass and labour productivity can be reduced. Along with illness, this affects wages and earnings. Studies have shown that a 1 percent increase in body mass index (BMI, a measure of weight for a given height) is associated with an increase in wages of more than 2 percent, at least over part of the range of BMIs.
- Micronutrient deficiencies can also reduce work capacity. Surveys suggest that anaemia caused by iron deficiency is associated with a 17 percent loss of productivity in heavy manual labour.
- Investment and risk-taking are essential for economic growth, but people who live on the edge of starvation are likely to be extremely cautious about investing, since they cannot afford a drop in production or earnings.
- All this means that widespread hunger can depress the performance of whole economies. Studies in Bangladesh, India, Pakistan and Viet Nam estimate that adult productivity losses due to the combined effect of stunting and deficiencies of iodine and iron considerably reduce the growth of incomes.

Growth in incomes is essential if under-nourishment is to be reduced, but it is not enough by itself. Better public services — such as improved female and nutrition education, safe drinking water and improved health services and sanitation — are also needed. Interventions in these areas must be carefully targeted towards the most vulnerable groups.

Agriculture holds the key

The development community today shares the same broad recipe for poverty reduction. The recipe involves fostering pro-poor economic growth and favouring poor people's access to all the services and other factors that support poverty eradication and define an acceptable standard of living: markets, credit and income-producing assets, basic education, health and sanitation services, safe water, transport and communications infrastructure, and so on. Providing access to these basic human rights is seen as an end in itself, but it will also boost economic growth.

Growth in the agricultural sector has a crucial role to play in reducing poverty. The International Fund for Agricultural Development (IFAD) estimates that seven out of ten of the world's poor still live in rural areas. They include smallholders, landless labourers, traditional pastoralists, artisanal fishers and marginalized groups such as refugees, indigenous peoples and female-headed households.

Many of the rural poor work directly in agriculture, as smallholders, farm labourers or herders. Their incomes can be boosted by

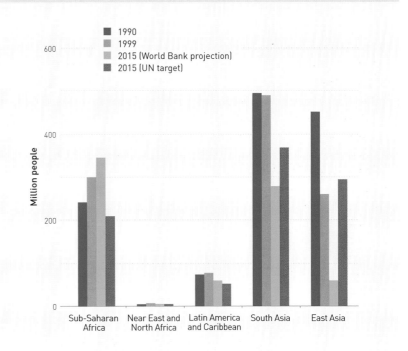

Progress in poverty alleviation: number of people living in poverty, 1990 to 2015

Legend:
- 1990
- 1999
- 2015 (World Bank projection)
- 2015 (UN target)

Y-axis: Million people (0, 200, 400, 600)

X-axis categories: Sub-Saharan Africa, Near East and North Africa, Latin America and Caribbean, South Asia, East Asia

Source: World Bank (2001b)

pro-poor measures, such as ensuring fair access to land, water and other assets and inputs, and to services, including education and health.

Agricultural growth spreads its benefits widely. Growth in the incomes of farmers and farm labourers creates increased demand for basic non-farm products and services in rural areas. These include tools, blacksmithing, carpentry, clothes, processed food bought from roadside kiosks, and so on. These goods and services are often difficult to trade over long distances. They tend to be produced and provided locally, usually with labour-intensive methods, and so have great potential to create employment and alleviate poverty. Surveys in four African countries have shown that between one-third and two-thirds of income increases in rural areas are spent on such local goods and services.

For the poor, the rural non-farm sector offers a relatively easy escape route from

> Income growth is essential if undernourishment is to be reduced, but better public services — improved female and nutrition education, safe drinking water, and improved health services and sanitation — are also crucial.

> Growth in agriculture and in associated rural non-farm employment can have a broad impact in reducing poverty in rural areas, where seven out of ten of the world's poor live.

poverty. Rural non-farm enterprise often requires little capital or training to set up and so offers many of the rural poor opportunities to find work and raise their incomes. Non-farm activities provide 44 percent of rural jobs in Asia and 25 percent in Latin America. In rural India they provide 60 percent of the income of the poorest 20 percent of the rural population.

But the rural non-farm sector cannot grow independently: agriculture must grow first, to generate the increased demand for non-farm products. There can be a general rise in local wages only when growth in both farm and non-farm activities has soaked up most of the pool of rural underemployment.

And agricultural growth alone may not always produce a decline in rural poverty. If landholdings are very unequal, increased incomes from farming may accrue almost entirely to large-scale farmers or absentee landlords, who may either save it or invest it outside the rural areas, on urban or imported goods. In such cases the impact of agricultural growth on poverty may be limited, and policies to reduce inequality of access to assets such as land, water and inputs will be needed instead.

What economic policies at national level foster agricultural growth in developing countries? During the 1950s and 1960s it was widely believed that only industrial growth could deliver economic development. As a result, industry was protected while agriculture was heavily taxed or afforded low priority. By the end of the 1970s, there was increasing emphasis on the structural reform of economies. It was hoped that privatization, the liberalization of internal and external trade, lower taxes and reduced government intervention would produce higher economic growth and reduce the bias against agriculture.

These measures have been widely adopted. However, there is little evidence to show that they have done much to increase growth, either in gross domestic product (GDP) as a whole or in agricultural GDP. This suggests that, badly needed though they were, these measures are not enough in themselves and need to be supplemented with other policies.

International trade and globalization

Freer trade is highly prized as a route to peace and prosperity. In developing countries, particularly in the least developed economies, freer trade in agriculture can raise incomes greatly, be an important source of foreign exchange and act as a catalyst for overall development. For most countries, food imports are already an important source of supplies and will continue to contribute to food security.

Rising agricultural trade deficits in developing countries

The trade patterns of developing countries have changed rapidly over the past 40 years:

- Agricultural exports have grown modestly compared to those of manufactured goods, resulting in a dramatic decline in the share of agricultural exports in total traded merchandise, from about 50 percent in the early 1960s to about 6 percent by the year 2000.
- The overall agricultural trade surplus of these countries has virtually disappeared and the outlook to 2030 suggests that they will become, as a group, net importers of agricultural commodities, especially of temperate-zone commodities.
- The least developed countries (LDCs), also as a group, became net importers of agricultural

Trade reform has lowered the barriers to trade, increased global economic integration, enhanced productivity and boosted incomes — and will continue to do so. Not all countries or stakeholders have been winners, but national and international policy interventions could soften the impact on losers. Special measures could ensure that a greater share of the benefits of trade go to developing countries.

from the developing world. These trade distortions impose high costs and create widespread inefficiencies. In the countries that use them, they exact higher prices and taxes from consumers and taxpayers. For other countries, they limit access to export markets and introduce unfair competition in domestic markets. They hold world commodity prices down and so hold back the development of agriculture, especially in developing countries where less government support is available.

On the market side, growth in agricultural exports from developing countries has been held back by sluggish and largely saturated demand in developed markets, in particular for tropical products such as coffee, cocoa and tea.

Ambitious goals, modest achievements

The benefits of trade reform experienced by many outward-oriented economies have created the momentum to continue reducing the barriers to trade. Many developing countries had already liberalized aspects of their agricultural trade since the 1980s under structural adjustment reforms. These reforms, and the full range of policies that affect agricultural trade, were subjected to systematic multilateral

products as early as the mid-1980s. Their agricultural trade deficit has been widening rapidly and could quadruple by 2030.

Both policy and market factors are driving these changes. On the policy side, barriers to trade and support for domestic production in the developed (mainly the OECD) countries have held back the growth of agricultural exports

Agricultural trade balance and share of agricultural exports in merchandise trade, 1960 to 2000

The surplus of developing countries has been shrinking...

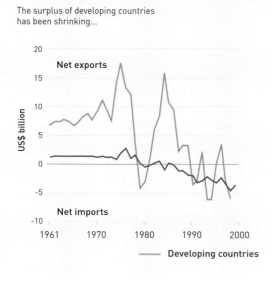

...as also has the share of agricultural exports in total merchandise trade

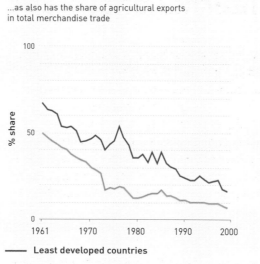

Developing countries ——— Least developed countries

Source: FAO data

controls for the first time by the Uruguay Round's 1994 Agreement on Agriculture (AoA).

The Agreement was hailed as a watershed, yet so far the results have been modest and often disappointing. FAO studies have found that, for most agricultural commodities, the AoA's impact on prices and levels of trade has been negligible, as has its impact on many developing economies. Producer support of all types remains high in developed countries: in 2000 it totalled US$245 billion in the OECD countries. This figure rises to US$327 billion if more general transfers to agriculture are included.

Tariffs continue to curb trade. Under the AoA, non-tariff barriers such as quotas were to be replaced by equivalent tariffs. In addition, developed countries agreed to reduce all their tariffs by an average of 36 percent, over a period of six years, with a minimum of 15 percent for any one trade item. Developing countries agreed to reduce tariffs by 24 percent over a ten-year period. The least developed countries were not required to make any reductions.

The reductions made since 1994 have complied with these goals, but it is not clear that market access has improved significantly. Developed country tariffs have been cut by an average 37 percent, but the deepest cuts have been mainly for unprocessed tropical crops that already had low tariffs. Commodities also produced in developed countries, and processed products, benefited much less. For example, maximum allowable tariffs agreed by the European Union (EU) under the AoA were 86 percent on beef and 215 percent on frozen beef, whereas they are only 6 percent on pineapples but 25 percent on processed pineapples.

Domestic support remains high. Government support for agriculture can also distort trade, by allowing domestic producers to sell at lower prices than would otherwise be economically viable.

The AoA also covered domestic support. Several types of support, such as research, infrastructure and environmental programmes, were exempted. Developing countries could also

exclude measures of a developmental nature, such as agricultural and rural development programmes.

The AoA required developed countries to make a 20 percent reduction in their support for agriculture, developing countries a 13.3 percent cut and least developed countries none. These cuts were to be made with reference to a 1986-88 base, over a period of six years for developed countries and ten years for developing countries.

In reality many countries have faced much less pressure to reduce support for, and protection of, their agricultural sector. This is mainly due to the fact that the commitments to liberalize were based on historically high levels of support and protection. These so-called "bound" levels remained high enough to maintain much of the protection previously enjoyed, even after the cuts had been implemented. Indeed, total support to agriculture in the rich OECD countries was actually higher in 1998-2000 than before the AoA.

Export subsidies are still substantial. The AoA brought direct subsidies for agricultural exports into an international trade agreement for the first time. Indirect subsidies, such as export credit guarantees and food aid, were also covered. Developed countries agreed to reduce their expenditure on subsidies by 36 percent and developing countries by 24 percent. Reductions in the volume of subsidized exports were also negotiated, with reductions for each commodity of 21 percent required for developed and 14 percent for developing countries. Least developed countries undertook no commitments to reduce their subsidies. The EU accounts for the bulk of direct export subsidies: in 1998 it spent US$5.8 billion, more than 90 percent of all such subsidies covered by the AoA.

More liberalization would mainly benefit developed countries

According to most studies, complete liberalization of agricultural trade could produce valuable overall welfare gains, but some groups would win while others would

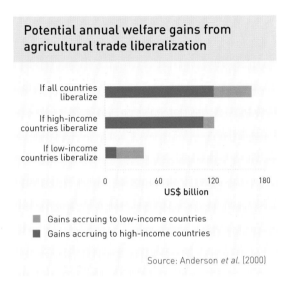

Potential annual welfare gains from agricultural trade liberalization

If all countries liberalize

If high-income countries liberalize

If low-income countries liberalize

0   60   120   180

US$ billion

- Gains accruing to low-income countries
- Gains accruing to high-income countries

Source: Anderson *et al.* (2000)

lose. The benefits would go mainly to consumers and taxpayers in industrial countries, where agriculture is most protected, and to developing country agricultural exporters. In contrast, urban and landless rural consumers in developing countries might end up paying higher prices for some foodstuffs, especially cereals, milk, meat and sugar. Specific measures would be needed to help such loser groups.

The results of studies on the impact of agricultural trade liberalization vary according to the assumptions they make. For example, a recent study found that complete liberalization would boost global incomes by US$165 billion a year. The largest benefits would arise from reforms in developed countries, but the lion's share of these, amounting to some US$121 billion, would also remain in these countries. Developing countries stand to gain significantly (by US$31 billion) only if they also liberalize their own trade.

The current FAO study also looked at the impacts of gradually removing price supports and other subsidies over the 30 years to 2030. The analysis focused on the expected price effects for consumers and producers, in both developed and developing countries. It found that international prices could rise moderately, while prices would fall substantially in countries with high levels of protection. Producers trading at international prices would gain, while those

producing at inflated protected prices would lose. Like the study described above, the FAO study found that the benefits for consumers in hitherto protected OECD markets could be high, but it also stressed that high processing and distribution costs in these countries could mean that lower prices for raw products would not translate into substantially lower prices for the final consumer. Consumers in developing countries, where processing and distribution margins are much smaller, stood to lose more significantly. Trade liberalization would not change the main conclusion of this study, that developing countries will increasingly become net importers of agricultural products — but it would slow the process somewhat.

Why do developing countries stand to gain so much less from trade liberalization than developed countries? One reason is that many developing countries have become net importers of agricultural products, and modest increases in world prices are unlikely to turn them into net exporters. In the importing developing countries, consumers stand to lose more from freer trade than domestic producers are likely to gain.

The finding that gains for producers in developing countries would often be small reflects a number of factors:

- Many studies show that a cut in OECD subsidies would merely bring about an exchange of market shares between OECD countries. This is because OECD trade distortions are concentrated on temperate-zone commodities — products for which, in the majority of developing countries, the production potential is limited more by agro-ecological conditions than by policy distortions abroad.

Eliminating all agricultural policy distortions could produce global annual welfare gains of up to US$165 billion, of which three-quarters would go to developed countries.

- Where developing countries have a comparative advantage — in such commodities as coffee, cocoa, tea, spices and tropical fruits — developed countries' import tariffs have already been reduced and the effects of further liberalization are likely to be small.
- Higher and more stable international prices are not always transmitted to farmers in developing countries. Inadequate infrastructure and inefficient marketing systems insulate many of them from world markets.
- Farmers in developing countries may not gain as long as domestic policies largely offset the price incentives from international markets. Most developing countries heavily taxed their agriculture throughout the 1970s and 1980s; many, including India, China and Pakistan, continued to do so during the 1990s.

How can trade liberalization benefit developing countries?

What measures and strategies would ensure that the poorest and most vulnerable countries and population groups receive an equitable share of the benefits of trade liberalization? The aim should be to:

- Eliminate direct and indirect export subsidies.
- Rationalize and simplify access to OECD markets. Specifically, rationalize and simplify trade preferences, assist countries whose preferences have been eroded through multilateral liberalization, and deepen existing preferences for very poor countries.
- Reduce OECD tariffs and consumer taxes on processed agricultural products, with special preferences for products from developing countries.
- Eliminate tariff escalation for tropical commodities, in the developing as well as the developed countries. Tariffs are rising even faster in the former than in the latter group. The purchasing power of China's or India's rapidly growing middle class could turn these countries into major importers of some tropical agricultural products over the next 30 years.
- Create or expand safety nets and food distribution schemes, to ensure that low-income consumers are not penalized by rises in the prices of food imports.

If developing countries are to benefit from freer trade, their farmers will need to become more responsive to the rising and more stable international prices that should result from such trade. A massive mobilization of resources is needed to improve agricultural productivity at home and thus competitiveness abroad. The most important measures are increased credits for rural areas, and more investment in all aspects of support for agricultural production and processing, including rural infrastructure (irrigation, transportation, storage and marketing), research, education and training, and standard setting and quality control.

Substantial gains would also result from other policy reforms. In developing countries, removing taxes on agricultural exports and tariffs on non-agricultural imports (machinery, fertilizers and pesticides) would improve the terms of agricultural trade and help farmers compete on international markets. In developed countries, removing trade barriers in labour-intensive manufacturing could bring benefits for farmers in developing countries. For example, a rapidly growing textile industry would create new income opportunities for cotton farmers in the tropics.

Non-agricultural exports now account for more than 90 percent of the total exports from developing countries, and more than 80 percent in the case of least developed countries. Deeper and broader preferential access to the markets for manufactured goods in some developed countries could make an important contribution to food security in the least developed countries, providing them with the means to finance their huge and rapidly increasing food import needs in the future.

Does globalization disadvantage the poorest countries?

Globalization is a modern word for a process that has been going on for centuries. New technologies in the fields of transport and communications, from advances in sailing and navigation to the steamship and the telegraph, have often reduced the cost of shifting goods around the world in the past, leading to increased economic integration. Recently, such technologies have included roll-on roll-off container systems and the Internet, while lower trade barriers have further eased the movement of goods and capital.

Globalization has brought lower prices to consumers, and investment and employment to newly industrializing countries. But it has also raised widespread public concern over the fate of the poorer developing countries, which are alleged to have been left further and further behind as the rest of the world advances.

There is strong evidence that countries can be disadvantaged in the global marketplace by their geographical endowments. Lack of infrastructure can make it hard to get perishable products to markets, increasing marketing costs and so deterring investment. As new investment heads for better-endowed

areas, those countries and regions with physical and infrastructural handicaps may be bypassed, falling further and further behind and finding themselves trapped in a vicious circle of disadvantage.

Most poor countries are located in the tropics, where the higher incidence of crop and livestock diseases and pests and excessive or inadequate rainfall are further factors compromising their ability to participate in global agricultural markets. Distance from the sea and a lack of navigable waterways can constitute additional disadvantages. Outside Europe, average incomes in landlocked countries are only a third of those in countries with a seaboard.

Sub-Saharan Africa, located mainly in the tropics and with a high proportion of problematic soils, suffers multiple handicaps in the global marketplace. Only 21 percent of this region's population live within 100 km of the coast or of a navigable river, against 89 percent in high-income countries. The proportion of the population that is landlocked is seven times higher than in rich countries. Landlocked countries in Africa have average freight costs almost three times higher than in high-income countries.

In contrast, regions of the United States, Western Europe and temperate-zone East Asia within 100 km of a coastline account for a mere 3 percent of the world's inhabited land area. Yet they house 13 percent of the world's population and produce at least 32 percent of the world's GDP.

Combining data on population and income levels provides a revealing picture of the distribution or density of incomes over different countries and regions. It underscores the importance of infrastructure and/or geographical location, showing that:
- Nearly all landlocked countries in the world are poor, except for a few in Western and Central Europe which are deeply integrated into the regional European market and connected by multiple low-cost trade routes.
- Coastal regions, and regions linked to coasts by navigable waterways, are strongly favoured relative to the hinterlands.

The conditions for market integration differ vastly across regions

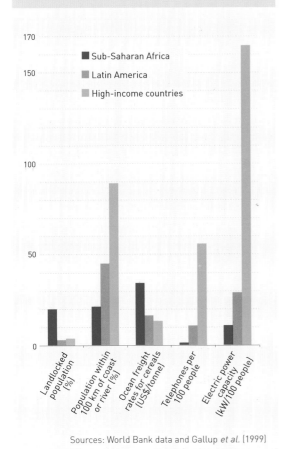

- ■ Sub-Saharan Africa
- ■ Latin America
- High-income countries

Sources: World Bank data and Gallup *et al.* (1999)

- Sub-Saharan Africa stands out as the region that is most disadvantaged in terms of unfavourable agro-ecological conditions as well as inadequate transport and communications infrastructure.

Does globalization concentrate too much power in the hands of multinationals?

Globalization is often charged with shifting power away from national governments to multinational enterprises (MNEs). MNEs have been accused of abusing market power, exploiting farmers and labourers around the world, and exerting pressure on governments to reduce environmental and labour standards.

Today MNEs in food and agriculture operate across many country borders. They are more and more vertically integrated, covering the whole sequence of operations from producing and marketing seeds, through purchasing the crop, to food processing and distribution.

When they control large parts of the supply chain, these large corporations can exert monopoly selling or buying power, thereby putting pressure on farmers and retailers. Through production contracts or joint ownership in land or livestock operations, they can tie farmers into buying the company's inputs and selling their produce only to the company. Farmers may also lose entrepreneurial capacity and become more or less dependent workers on their own farms. It is also true that MNEs can and do move operations from country to country in search of lower costs, including wage rates, and of lower labour and environmental standards.

Benefits of globalization

However, if the often heard demands for global parity in wages and environmental standards were met, this would remove a major competitive advantage of poorer countries and could halt the flow of investment towards them, seriously prejudicing their further development.

Countries that excluded MNEs would be excluding the best available channels for getting their products to the global marketplace. MNEs usually upgrade local skills, methods, standards and technologies as they expand in a country. For example, in the late 1980s, in China's Heilongjiang province, the multinational Nestlé built rural roads, organized milk collection points and trained dairy farmers in basic animal health and hygiene.

MNEs also force local firms to upgrade in order to remain competitive. Recent research shows that the greater the degree of openness of a national industry to foreign competitors, the greater its productivity. Indeed, the presence of foreign firms may be the single greatest stimulus to improving productivity available in many developing country settings.

The claim is often made that globalization makes the world's poor poorer, but there is no evidence for this. Countries may, however, become poorer in a relative sense as they fail to

Sprawling giants

Growing concentration has led to a situation in which just four companies based in the United States and linked in two alliances — Cargill/Monsanto and Novartis/ADM — control over 80 percent of the world market for seeds and 75 percent of that for agrochemicals.

Another United States giant, ConAgra, is one of the three largest flour millers in North America. It produces its own livestock feed. It ranks third in cattle feeding and second in slaughtering, third in pork processing and fourth in broiler production. Through United Agri Products, it sells agrochemicals and seeds around the world. It owns the important grain trading company, Peavey. It is second only to Philip Morris as a leading food processor and sells processed foods through brands such as Armour, Swift and Hunt's.

Income density in the world

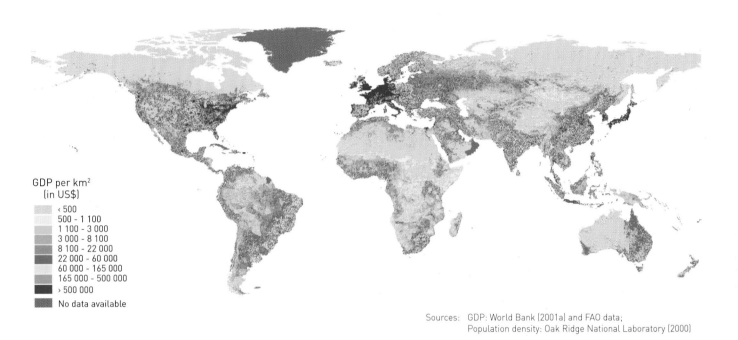

GDP per km² (in US$)

- < 500
- 500 – 1 100
- 1 100 – 3 000
- 3 000 – 8 100
- 8 100 – 22 000
- 22 000 – 60 000
- 60 000 – 165 000
- 165 000 – 500 000
- > 500 000
- No data available

Sources: GDP: World Bank (2001a) and FAO data;
Population density: Oak Ridge National Laboratory (2000)

benefit from globalization. Recent research conducted for the World Bank suggests that openness to international trade boosts economic growth. Developing countries with policies that favour openness increased their rate of GDP growth from 1 percent in the 1960s to 3 percent in the 1970s, 4 percent in the 1980s and 5 percent in the 1990s. In contrast, much of the rest of the developing world, containing about 2 billion people, is becoming increasingly marginalized. The aggregate growth rate of these countries was actually negative in the 1990s.

Overall, the benefits of continuing globalization are likely to outweigh the risks and costs. Negative impacts can be mitigated by appropriate policies. A combination of measures

> Multinational enterprises often upgrade local skills, methods, standards and technologies as they expand in a country. In so doing, they force local firms to upgrade in order to remain competitive.

including openness, investments in infrastructure, the promotion of economic integration and limits on market concentration and control, could make globalization work for the benefit for the poor.

31

Prospects by Major Sector

Crop production

Cereals: an extra billion tonnes needed

The 1990s saw a decline in the growth of world cereal consumption. This was due not to limits in production capacity but rather to slower growth in demand, partly caused by exceptional and largely transient factors. Growth in consumption will resume, leading to growing dependence on imports in developing countries. The potential exists for traditional and new exporters to fill this gap, but problems of food security and environmental degradation will need to be addressed.

Cereals are still by far the world's most important sources of food, both for direct human consumption and indirectly, as inputs to livestock production. What happens in the cereal sector is therefore crucial to world food supplies.

Since the mid-1960s the world has managed to raise cereal production by almost a billion tonnes. Over the next 30 years it must do so again. Is the task within its capabilities?

Growth of cereal demand slows down
The growth rate of world demand for cereals fell to 1 percent a year in the 1990s, down from 1.9 percent in the 1980s and 2.5 percent in the 1970s. World annual cereal use per person

(including animal feeds) peaked in the mid-1980s at 334 kg and has since fallen to 317 kg (1997-99 average).

This rapid decline was thought by some to herald a new world food crisis. It was interpreted as a sign that the world was hitting the limits of its capacity for food production and would soon experience serious threats to food security.

In fact, average cereal consumption per person in developing countries has risen steadily throughout the past four decades. The slowdown in the growth of world consumption was due not to production constraints but to a series of factors that limited demand. Among these factors, some are ongoing and widespread:

- World population growth has been slowing.
- Many large countries, especially China, are reaching medium to high consumption levels, such that further rises will be much less rapid than in the past.
- Persistent poverty has prevented hundreds of millions of people from meeting their food needs.

Other factors, however, are largely transient. These include:

- A fall in demand in the transition economies. This was the strongest factor during the 1990s, when both consumption and imports in these countries fell from the very high levels they had reportedly reached earlier.
- The use of cereals for animal feeds in the EU declined until the early 1990s, as high domestic prices favoured cereal substitutes, which were largely imported. Growth in feed

use resumed after EU policy reforms lowered domestic prices.

- Consumption grew more slowly in oil-exporting countries after the effect of the initial boom in oil prices on incomes and cereal imports had largely dissipated.
- Demand grew more slowly in the second half of the 1990s in the East Asian economies, which were hit by economic crisis.

The influence of these transient factors is already on the wane. Over the next 15 years they will gradually cease depressing the growth in cereal demand, which is projected to recover, rising to 1.4 per cent a year by 2015.

Looking further ahead, slower population growth and the levelling off of food consumption in many countries will continue to dampen demand, the growth of which is expected to slow to 1.2 percent a year over the period 2015 to 2030. Nevertheless, the production task facing world agriculture is massive. By 2030, an extra billion tonnes of cereals will be needed each year. Unforeseeable events such as oil price booms, dramatic growth spurts or crises could, of course, alter effective demand over short periods, but will not greatly change the big picture.

Developing countries will become more dependent on imports

In the developing countries the demand for cereals has grown faster than production. The net cereal imports of these countries rose from 39 million tonnes a year in the mid-1970s to 103 million tonnes in 1997-99, representing a move from 4 percent of their annual cereal use to 9 percent. This dependence on imports is likely to increase in the years ahead. By 2030 the developing countries could be importing 265 million tonnes of cereals, or 14 percent of their consumption, annually.

Though this increase may seem massive, it represents a lower rate of growth over the next three decades than since the mid-1970s. If real food prices do not rise, and industry and services grow as previously, then most countries will be able to afford to import cereals to meet their needs. However, the poorest countries with the worst food

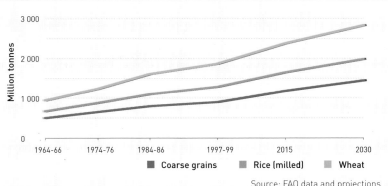

World demand for cereals, 1965 to 2030

Million tonnes

Source: FAO data and projections

Coarse grains ■ Rice (milled) ■ Wheat

The developing countries will become increasingly dependent on cereal imports. By 2030 they could be producing only 86 percent of their own needs, with net imports amounting to some 265 million tonnes annually — almost three times present levels.

security also tend to be least able to pay for imports.

Exporters can fill the gap

Can the rest of the world produce the export surpluses needed to fill the gap? It is worth examining the experience of the past quarter century. Between the mid-1970s and 1997-99 the net annual imports of all cereal-importing countries almost doubled, from 89 million tonnes to 167 million tonnes.

Cereal exporters coped well with the spurt in demand, doubling their export levels. Traditional exporters such as Australia, North America, Argentina and Uruguay played their part. They have the potential to continue to do so. But about half the total increase in exports came from a new player, the EU. From being a net importer of 21 million tonnes of grain a year in the mid-1970s, the EU became a net exporter of 24 million tonnes a year in 1997-99. Initially, much of this turnaround depended on heavy price support and protectionist policies. Various EU policy reforms have since brought domestic prices broadly into line with international prices, but the EU is likely to remain a significant net exporter even if its trade is further liberalized.

The transition economies are another possible source of future exports. Indeed, they are already moving into surplus. Spare land is plentiful in parts of Eastern Europe and Russia, and the scope for increasing productivity by reducing losses and raising yields is high. FAO's projections suggest that the transition countries could be net exporters of 10 million tonnes of cereals a year by 2015 and 25 million tonnes by 2030.

The transition countries became large net importers of cereals over the two decades to the early 1990s. They have since reversed this trend and could be net exporters of 10 million tonnes annually by 2015 and 25 million tonnes by 2030.

Prospects for key crops

Food staples

Wheat. The world's major cereal crop accounted for 31 percent of global cereal consumption in 1997-99. A growing share of wheat is used for animal feed in the industrial countries — 45 percent of total use in the EU. Wheat use per person in developing countries, overwhelmingly for food, has continued to rise, and most developing countries are increasingly dependent on imports. Among the net importers are some major wheat producers, such as Egypt, Islamic Republic of Iran, Mexico and Brazil. Over the coming years wheat consumption is expected to increase in all regions, including the transition countries as their consumption revives. In several rice-eating countries, increases in wheat consumption go hand in hand with constant or declining consumption of rice. The import

dependence of developing countries (excluding exporters Argentina and Uruguay) should continue to grow, with net wheat imports expected to rise from 72 millions tonnes a year in 1997-99 to 160 million tonnes in 2030.

Rice. This crop is overwhelmingly used for direct human consumption, and made up 21 percent of the world's cereal consumption by weight in 1997-99. Average consumption per person in developing countries has been levelling off since the mid-1980s, reflecting economic development and income growth in major East Asian countries. It has, however, been growing in some regions, including South Asia, where it is still low. Consumption is expected to grow more slowly in the future than in the past. Indeed, average consumption per person in developing countries may well start to decline during the period 2015 to 2030. This will ease pressures on production, but given the slow yield growth of recent years, maintaining even modest increases in production will be a challenge to research and irrigation policy.

Coarse grains. These include maize, sorghum, barley, rye, oats and millet, and some regionally important grains such as tef (Ethiopia) or quinoa (Bolivia and Ecuador). About three-fifths of world consumption of coarse grains is used for animal feed, but where food insecurity is high these crops remain very important in direct human consumption: in sub-Saharan Africa, 80 percent of the grain harvest is used in this way. Consumption of coarse grains has been rising fast, driven mainly by growing use as animal feed in developing countries. In the future, consumption may well grow faster than that of rice or wheat, in line with the growth of the livestock sector. Developing countries will account for a rising share of world production, from less than half at present to just under three-fifths by 2030.

Oilcrops. This sector has been one of the world's most dynamic in recent decades, growing at almost double the speed of world agriculture as a whole. It covers a wide range of crops used not only for oil but also for direct consumption, animal feeds and a number of industrial uses. Oil-palm, soybean, sunflower and rapeseed account for almost three-quarters of world oilseed production, but olive oil, groundnut, sesame and coconut are also significant. The rapid expansion of production has meant that oilcrops have accounted for a huge share of the expansion of the world's agricultural land, with a net increase of 75 million ha between 1974-76 and 1997-99 — this at a time when the area under cereals shrank by 28 million ha.

With their high energy content, oilcrops have played a key role in improving food energy supplies in developing countries. Just over one out of every five kilocalories added to consumption in the developing countries in the past two decades originated in this group of products. This trend looks set to continue and indeed intensify: 45 out of every 100 additional kilocalories in the period to 2030 may come from oilseeds. The rapid growth in consumption over the past few decades was accompanied by the emergence of several developing countries — China, India, Mexico and Pakistan, among others — as major and growing net importers of vegetable oils. The result has been that the traditional surplus of the vegetable oils/oilseeds complex in the balance of payments of the developing countries has turned into a deficit in recent years. This has happened despite the spectacular growth of exports from a few developing countries that have come to dominate the world export scene, namely Malaysia and Indonesia for palm oil and Brazil and Argentina for soybean. In most other developing countries, the trend towards increased imports can be expected to continue.

Roots, tubers and plantains. World consumption of these crops as human food has been on the decline, but for 19 countries — all of them in Africa — they still provide more than a fifth, and sometimes as much as half, of all food energy. Cassava predominates in humid Central and West Africa and in the United Republic of Tanzania and Madagascar, while plantains are most important in Rwanda and cassava and sweet potato in West Africa and Burundi. Since most of these countries have low food consumption overall — less than 2 200 kcal per person per day — these crops play a crucial role in food security. In the period to 1997-99, Ghana and Nigeria made considerable advances in food security through the increased production of these crops, but in most of the other 17 countries per capita consumption stagnated or declined. The decline in world consumption of traditional roots and tubers has

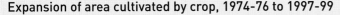

Expansion of area cultivated by crop, 1974-76 to 1997-99

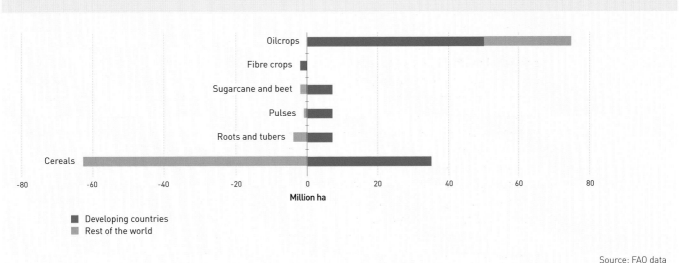

Million ha

■ Developing countries
■ Rest of the world

Source: FAO data

been accompanied by a gradual shift towards potato in some areas. A large part of this trend is explained by China, where millions of farmers and consumers have switched from sweet potato to potato.

Average demand for roots, tubers and plantains is projected to rise again in developing countries, with sweet potato and potato becoming particularly important as animal feeds. During the 1990s the use of imported cassava as feed in the EU skyrocketed because of high domestic prices for cereals, only to fall as reform of the Common Agricultural Policy reduced cereal prices. Cassava production for export as feed has been a major factor in expansion of the area cultivated in such countries as Thailand, a trend that is often associated with deforestation.

Traditional export crops

Beyond these basic food crops, the agriculture and often the whole economy of many developing countries depend to a high degree on the production of one or a few commodities destined principally for export. In this category are commodities such as banana, sugar, natural rubber and tropical beverages (tea, coffee and cocoa).

The distinction between export crops and those for the domestic market is not always neat, either across or even within the developing countries. For example, sugar is the export crop *par excellence* for Mauritius and Cuba but a major import for Egypt, Indonesia and several other countries. Vegetable oils and oilseeds (especially palm oil and soybean) are major and rapidly growing export crops for several countries (including Malaysia, Indonesia, Argentina and Brazil), but are heavily imported by countries such as India and China. Coffee and cocoa share the characteristic of being produced exclusively in the developing countries but consumed predominantly in the industrial ones. Natural rubber used to belong to this category, but more of it is now consumed in the developing countries (half of world consumption, up from a quarter in the mid-1970s) as they industrialize. Cotton is in the same class, but more so, with the developing countries having

turned into large net importers following the growth of their textiles industries and exports.

The economies of countries dependent on exports of these commodities are subject to changing conditions in the world market. Slow growth in world demand, combined with increasing supplies from the main producing and exporting countries, which compete with one another, have led to declining and widely fluctuating prices in the markets for several commodities. This has been particularly marked for coffee in recent years: per capita consumption in the industrial countries, accounting for two-thirds of world consumption, has been nearly constant for two decades, at around 4.5 kg, while production has increased, with several new countries, such as Viet Nam, entering the market. The result is that the price of Robusta coffee has nosedived, falling to US$0.50 per kg by January 2002, one-fifth of what it was in the mid-1990s.

For sugar and a few other commodities experiencing faster growth in consumption, mainly in the developing countries, the earnings of developing country exporters have been curbed by policies restricting access to markets, including policies favouring substitute sweeteners such as corn syrup. Such policies are very common in the main industrial countries that are, or used until recently to be, large importers. The EU used policies of this kind to turn itself from a large net importer, which it was until the second half of the 1970s, into a large net exporter today.

Looking into the future, the scope for growth in world demand and in the exports of developing countries is greatest for those commodities whose consumption is growing fairly rapidly in the developing countries themselves, several of which are likely to become large importers. In this category belong sugar and vegetable oils and, to a lesser extent, natural rubber and tea. Banana and cocoa are also becoming substantial import items in several developing countries, a trend that should intensify in the coming decades. In these two commodities, but also in others such as citrus and fruits and vegetables in general, there is still scope for growth in consumption

The scares that went away

Two countries, China and India, have been the focus of fears that the world might run into serious food shortages. Together they are home to over a third of the world's population.

Some analysts feared that China would become a permanent importer on an ever-increasing scale. This would raise food prices on the world market, reducing the ability of other poor countries and people to buy food.

China (not including Taiwan Province) was a large importer of cereals in most years up to 1991, with typical net imports of 5 to 15 million tonnes a year. However, in the 1990s the country turned this situation around. In all but two of the eight years from 1992 to 1999, China was a net exporter of cereals, even while domestic use rose from 295 to 310 kg per person per year.

In the 1960s and early 1970s it became commonplace to warn of impending famine in India and in South Asia as a whole. In the mid-1960s the region imported 10 million tonnes of cereals a year — 11 percent of its consumption — but even so its cereal use per person was low, only 146 kg per year.

Thirty-three years on, the region's population had doubled and cereal use had risen to 163 kg per person per year. Yet thanks to the green revolution, imports were only a third of their mid-1960s levels, running at less than 2 percent of consumption. India had become a small net exporter in most years since the late 1970s. However, per capita use is still low in the region, reflecting, among other things, the persistence of widespread poverty and the very low use of cereals as feed, given the low consumption of meat. If consumption had grown faster, it is an open question whether imports would have been contained at such low levels.

and imports in the industrial countries. In parallel, the transition economies will play a growing role as importers of tropical products, a process already under way. In contrast, the high concentration of coffee markets in the industrial countries, together with negligible growth in population and per capita consumption here, do not augur well for the expansion of production and exports in this commodity: a continuation of the current slow growth, of no more than 1.2 percent yearly, seems the most likely outcome.

In conclusion, the agriculture, overall economy and food security of several developing countries will continue to depend on several crops for which the world market conditions are not only volatile but also, on balance, on a declining trend as regards real prices. These characteristics of the market could be highly

China: from net importer to net exporter of cereals

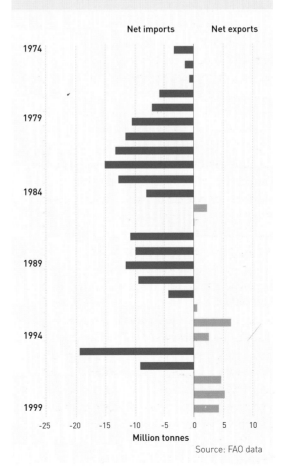

Source: FAO data

detrimental to the development prospects of these countries. Countries that have failed in the past to diversify their economies and reduce their dependence on these traditional export crops have had a growth record well below average. Their challenge is to change this scenario in the future. The experiences of countries such as Malaysia suggest that this can be done.

The environmental issues must be addressed
A frequently voiced concern is that the additional production required to meet world demand will be unsustainable, involving deepening levels of environmental damage that will undermine the natural resource base.

In the developed countries this concern relates mainly to the increased use of fertilizers and other chemical inputs. Past increases have led to serious problems of water and air pollution, and so will future ones unless counter-measures are taken.

Although the overuse of pesticides and other chemical inputs is a problem in some high-potential areas, increasing production in the developing world for the most part entails environmental risks of a different kind:
- In extensive farming and ranching systems, the major risks are soil erosion, soil mining and deforestation, leading to declining yields and desertification.
- In intensive irrigated farming systems, the major risks are salinization, waterlogging and water scarcities.

Some methods for increasing and sustaining crop production while minimizing environmental damage are already known and practised in some areas. Such methods need to be researched and extended for all environments, with appropriate policies that will encourage their rapid spread also being devised and implemented.

Land, water and crop yields

Although future demand for food and cash crops will grow more slowly than in the past, meeting this demand will still require the continued expansion of farmland, together with improvements in yield based on new plant varieties and farming technologies.

Questions have been raised about all of these factors. Is there enough suitable land and water to expand the rainfed and irrigated area as much as will be needed, or is the world running short of these vital inputs? Is there scope for the higher yields that will be required, or are yields approaching limits that cannot be breached? Can biotechnology deliver a new generation of higher-yielding crops better suited to difficult environments? And are there approaches to farming that can increase and sustain production while improving conservation? The following sections will examine these questions.

The sources of production growth

Increases in crop production derive from three main sources: expansion of arable land, increases in cropping intensity (the frequency with which crops are harvested from a given area) and improvements in yield.

Since the early 1960s, yield improvements have been by far the largest source of increase in world crop production, accounting for almost four-fifths or 78 percent of the increase between 1961 and 1999. A further 7 percent of the increase came from increased cropping intensity, while a mere 15 percent came from expansion of the arable area.

Yield improvement was by far the largest factor not just in the developed world but also in the developing countries, where it accounted for

70 percent of increased production. Expansion of the area cultivated accounted for just under a quarter of production growth in these countries. However, in areas with more abundant land, area expansion was a larger contributing factor. This was especially the case in sub-Saharan Africa, where it accounted for 35 percent, and in Latin America, where the figure reached 46 percent.

The projections suggest that these broad trends for the developing countries will continue, at least until 2030: land expansion is expected to account for 20 percent of production growth, yield improvements for about 70 percent and increased cropping intensity for the remainder. In sub-Saharan Africa and Latin America, land expansion will still be important, but it is likely to be increasingly outweighed by yield increases.

The FAO study indicates that, for the world as a whole, there is enough unused productive potential, in terms of land, water and yield improvements, to meet the expected growth in effective demand. However, this is a global

In future, 80 percent of increased crop production in developing countries will have to come from intensification: higher yields, increased multiple cropping and shorter fallow periods.

conclusion and there are several strong qualifications to bear in mind:
- Effective demand expresses people's purchasing power rather than the real need for food: wealthy consumers may indulge to excess, while the very poor may not be able to afford even basic foods.
- Data suggesting that food is getting cheaper may be flawed, because they do not reflect the environmental costs of expanding and intensifying agriculture; moreover, the failure to internalize resource costs may curb investment in agricultural research, holding back the potential for future growth in yields.
- Land or water scarcities and other problems will most certainly continue to arise at country and local levels, with serious consequences for poverty and food security.

Sources of growth in production, 1961 to 1999

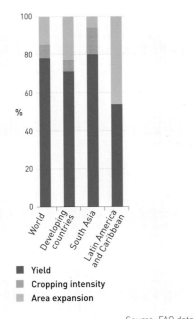

%

- ■ Yield
- ■ Cropping intensity
- ■ Area expansion

Source: FAO data

Land resources

Is there enough potential cropland for future needs?
It is often suggested that the world may be heading towards shortages of suitable agricultural land. FAO studies suggest that this will not be the case at the global level, although in some regions and areas there are already serious shortages, and these may worsen.

Less new agricultural land will be opened up than in the past. Over the period 1961-63 to 1997-99 the expansion of arable land in developing countries totalled 172 million ha, an increase of 25 percent. In the next 30 years an increase of only 120 million ha, or 13 percent, will be required. Adding an extra 3.75 million ha

Fears of an imminent crunch between population growth and land availability are unwarranted. Most future growth in crop production will stem from improved yields. In some countries, however, land shortages may bite.

a year may seem a daunting task — but it is less than the rate of 4.8 million ha a year that was actually achieved over the period 1961-63 to 1997-99. A slowdown in expansion is expected in all regions, but this is mainly a reflection of the slower growth in demand for crops.

There is still potential agricultural land that is as yet unused. At present some 1.5 billion ha of land is used for arable and permanent crops, around 11 percent of the world's surface area. A new assessment by FAO and the International Institute for Applied Systems Analysis (IIASA) of soils, terrains and climates compared with the needs of and for major crops suggests that a further 2.8 billion ha are to some degree suitable for rainfed production. This is almost twice as much as is currently farmed.

Of course, much of this potential land is in practice unavailable, or locked up in other valuable uses. Some 45 percent is covered in forests, 12 percent is in protected areas and

3 percent is taken up by human settlements and infrastructure. In addition, much of the land reserve may have characteristics that make agriculture difficult, such as low soil fertility, high soil toxicity, high incidence of human and animal diseases, poor infrastructure, and hilly or otherwise difficult terrain.

The pool of unused suitable cropland is very unevenly distributed. By the end of the twentieth century, sub-Saharan Africa and Latin America were still farming only around a fifth of their potentially suitable cropland. More than half the remaining global land balance was in just seven countries in these two regions: Angola, Argentina, Bolivia, Brazil, Colombia, Democratic Republic of Congo and the Sudan. At the other extreme, in the Near East and North Africa 87 percent of suitable land was already being farmed, while in South Asia the figure was no less than 94 percent. In a few countries of the Near East and North Africa, the land balance is negative – that is, more land is being cropped than is suitable for rainfed cropping. This is possible where, for example, land that is too sloping or too dry for rainfed crops has been brought into production by terracing or irrigation.

More than 80 percent of the projected expansion in arable area is expected to take place in sub-Saharan Africa and Latin America. Although there is still surplus land in these regions, the expansion may involve cutting back on long rotation and fallow periods. If fertilizer

Cropland in use and total suitable land (million ha)

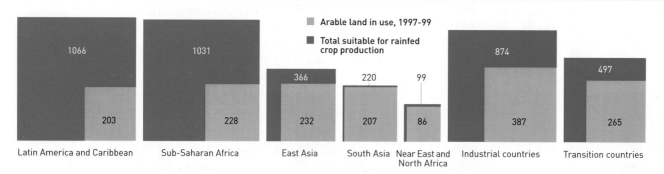

Arable land in use, 1997-99

Total suitable for rainfed crop production

Latin America and Caribbean	1066 / 203	
Sub-Saharan Africa	1031 / 228	
East Asia	366 / 232	
South Asia	220 / 207	
Near East and North Africa	99 / 86	
Industrial countries	874 / 387	
Transition countries	497 / 265	

Sources: FAO data and Fischer *et al.* (2000)

use does not rise to compensate, this may result in soil mining and stagnant or declining yields.

In contrast, in South Asia and the Near East and North Africa, where almost all suitable land is already in use, there will be next to no expansion in area. By 2030 the Near East and North Africa will be using 94 percent of its suitable cropland, with a remaining surplus of only 6 million ha. In South Asia the situation will be even tighter, with 98 percent already in

> The projections suggest that the arable area in developing countries will increase by almost 13 percent or 120 million ha over the years from 1997-99 to 2030.

cultivation. In South and East Asia, more than 80 percent of the increase in production will have to come from yield increases, since only 5 or 6 percent can come from expansion of the arable area.

Cropping intensities will rise in all developing regions, on average from 93 percent to 99 percent. This will occur through the shortening of fallow periods and increased multiple cropping, made possible partly by growth in the irrigated area.

Is land becoming scarcer?
There is widespread concern that the world may be running out of agricultural land. The trend towards scarcity associated with population growth is aggravated by the conversion of farmland to urban uses, by land degradation and by other factors.

Certainly, much farmland is being taken over for non-agricultural uses. Assuming a requirement for housing and other infrastructure of 40 ha per 1000 people, then world population growth between 1995 and 2030 implies the need for an additional 100 million ha of such non-agricultural land. Since most urban centres are sited on fertile agricultural land in coastal

plains or river valleys, when they expand they take up more of this prime land. In China alone, more than 2 million ha were taken out of agriculture in the ten years to1995.

Despite these losses, there is little evidence to suggest that global land scarcities lie ahead. Between the early 1960s and the late 1990s, world cropland grew by only 11 percent, while world population almost doubled. As a result, cropland per person fell by 40 percent, from 0.43 ha to only 0.26 ha. Yet, over this same period, nutrition levels improved considerably and the real price of food declined.

The explanation for this paradox is that productivity growth reduced the amount of land needed to produce a given amount of food by around 56 percent over this same period. This reduction, made possible by increases in yields and cropping intensities, more than matched the decline in area per person, allowing food production to increase.

Land scarcity and the problems associated with it do of course exist at country and local levels, with serious consequences for poverty and food security. In many places these are likely to worsen unless remedial action is taken.

How serious is land degradation?
Land degradation is the process by which the soil's current or future capacity to produce is lowered by chemical, physical or biological changes. Some analysts claim that accelerating land degradation will offset productivity improvements, while others believe the seriousness of this problem has been greatly overstated.

The truth is that the area of degraded land is not known with much precision. Its assessment is often based on expert judgement rather than objective measurement. For India alone, estimates by different public authorities vary from 53 million ha right up to 239 million ha.

The most comprehensive survey to date, the Global Assessment of Land Degradation (GLASOD), is now over ten years old. GLASOD estimated that a total of 1964 million ha were degraded, 910 million ha to at least a moderate degree (with significantly reduced productivity) and 305 million ha strongly or extremely so (no

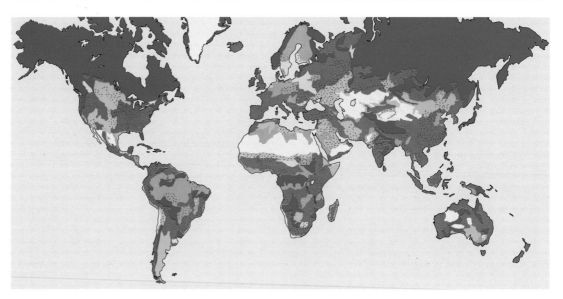

Human-induced soil degradation in the world

Soil degradation types

- Water erosion
- Wind erosion
- Chemical deterioration
- Physical deterioration
- Severe degradation

Other symbols

- Stable terrain
- Non-used wasteland
- Water bodies

Source: Oldeman *et al.* (1991)

longer suitable for agriculture). Water erosion was the most common problem, affecting almost 1 100 million ha, followed by wind erosion, which affected almost 600 million ha.

The impact of degradation on productivity is also hard to assess. Its seriousness varies widely from site to site over even small distances, and at the same site according to local weather, vegetation and farming techniques. Degradation is a slow process that can be masked by applying additional fertilizer or by changing the crops grown. GLASOD reported in 1991 that almost all farmland in China was degraded, yet between the early 1960s and mid-1990s China tripled her rice production and increased her wheat production sevenfold. Some studies suggest annual average losses in cropland productivity may be quite small, averaging only 0.2 to 0.4 percent a year.

Degradation also has off-site costs, such as the siltation of streambeds and dams, flood damage, loss of fisheries and the eutrophication of lakes and coastal waters. These costs are often greater than on-site costs. However, the off-site effects of degradation are not all negative: losses in one place may result in gains elsewhere, as when soil eroded from uplands boosts productivity in the alluvial plains where it is deposited.

Because it is difficult to quantify, the future progress of land degradation was not taken into account in the projections made for this study. However, some projected or foreseeable trends, driven primarily by economic forces, will tend to reduce its extent and impact:

- About a third of the harvested area in developing countries in 2030 is expected to be irrigated land, which is generally flat, protected by bunds and little affected by

Principal types of land degradation

- *Sloping land* is particularly prone to water erosion, especially in wet areas where slopes exceed 10 to 30 percent and conservation measures are lacking. In Nepal, for example, some 20 to 50 tonnes of soil per ha are estimated to be eroded each year from fields in the hills and mountains, while up to 200 tonnes per ha per year may be lost in some highly degraded watersheds. Crop yields in these areas fell by 8 to 21 percent in the 25 years to 1995. Around 45 percent of the world's agricultural land has slopes of more than 8 percent, and out of this total 9 percent has very steep slopes of over 30 percent.
- *Desertification*, a term referring to land degradation in arid and semi-arid areas, received a great deal of attention during the 1970s and 1980s, when it was believed that deserts such as the Sahara were spreading irreversibly. Estimates suggested that up to 70 percent of the world's 3.6 billion ha of drylands were degraded. Since then remote sensing has established that desert margins ebb and flow with natural climate changes, while studies on the ground are showing the resilience of crop and livestock systems and the adaptiveness of farmers and herders.

- *Salinization* occurs in irrigated areas, usually when inadequate drainage causes salts to concentrate in the upper soil layers where plants root. It is a problem mainly in the arid and semi-arid zones, where 10 to 50 percent of the irrigated area may be affected. Salinization can cause yield decreases of 10 to 25 percent for many crops and may prevent cropping altogether when it is severe. It is estimated that 3 percent of the world's agricultural land is affected. In East Asia, however, the proportion is 6 percent and in South Asia 8 percent. For the arid and semi-arid tropics as a whole, 12 percent of agricultural land may be affected.
- *Nutrient mining* is also a serious problem. Farmers often use insufficient fertilizer to replace the nitrogen, phosphorus and potassium (NPK) harvested with their crops and lost through leaching, while trace elements, such as iron or boron, may also be deficient. A detailed study of Latin America and the Caribbean found nutrient depletion in all areas and for almost all crops except beans. Net NPK losses in the region in 1993-95 amounted to 54 kg per ha per year. Another study suggested net losses of 49 kg per ha per year in sub-Saharan Africa.

erosion. A quarter of the rainfed land by that time will have slopes of less than 5 degrees, also generally not prone to heavy erosion.
- The shift in livestock production to more intensive systems will take some pressure off dryland pastures. However, in the developing countries this will be partly offset by the encroachment of cropland, which will reduce the area remaining for extensive grazing.
- As people leave rural areas for urban centres, and farming for non-farming occupations, steep slopes and other marginal land will tend to be abandoned and will revert to scrub and

forest. This process has already occurred rapidly in some European countries. In Italy, some 1.5 million ha were abandoned in the 1960s, 70 percent of which was sloping land. In some provinces, agricultural land decreased by 20 percent.

Other trends tending to reduce land degradation are likely, but their extent and intensity will depend heavily on the spread of improved agricultural and conservation practices, without which land degradation may worsen in many areas. The main practices and their potential impact are:

- No-till/conservation agriculture (NT/CA), which can maintain year-round soil cover and increase organic matter in soils, thereby reducing water and wind erosion.
- Increased fertilizer consumption and more efficient fertilizer use, which will reduce erosion by increasing root growth and ground cover.
- The use of irrigation, water harvesting, drought-tolerant crops and grazing-tolerant grasses, which will improve crop and vegetation cover and reduce erosion in drylands.
- The cultivation of legumes, which can add nitrogen to soils and improve their stability and texture in mixed crop-livestock farming systems.

Irrigation and water resources

A large share of the world's crops is already produced under irrigation. In 1997-99, irrigated land made up only about one-fifth of the total arable area in developing countries. However, because of higher yields and more frequent crops, it accounted for two-fifths of all crop production and close to three-fifths of cereal production.

This share is expected to increase further in the next three decades. Based on the potential for irrigation, national plans for the sector and the moisture needs of crops, the developing countries as a whole can be expected to expand their irrigated area from 202 million ha in 1997-99 to 242 million ha by 2030. This is a net projection – that is, it is based on the

There will be no overall shortage of land or water for irrigation, but serious problems will persist in some countries and regions.

assumption that land lost due, for example, to salinization and water shortages will be compensated by rehabilitation or by the substitution of new areas.

Most of this expansion will occur in land-scarce areas where irrigation is already crucial: South Asia and East Asia, for example, will add 14 million ha each. The Near East and North Africa will also see significant expansion. In land-abundant sub-Saharan Africa and Latin America, where both the need and the potential for irrigation are lower, the increase is expected to be much more modest – 2 million and 4 million ha respectively.

Although the projected expansion is ambitious, it is much less daunting than what has already been achieved. Since the early 1960s, no less than 100 million ha of new irrigated land have been created. The net increase projected for the next three decades is only 40 percent of that. The expected annual growth rate of 0.6 percent is less than a third of the rate achieved over the past 30 years.

The FAO study did not make projections for irrigation in the developed countries, which account for around a quarter of the world's irrigated area. Irrigation in this group of countries grew very rapidly in the 1970s, but by the 1990s the pace of growth had slowed to only 0.3 percent per year.

Is there enough irrigable land for future needs? As with land in general, it has been suggested that the world may soon experience shortages of land suitable for irrigation. There is concern, too, that vast areas of presently irrigated land may be severely damaged by salinization. Once again, at global level these fears seem exaggerated, though serious problems may occur at local level.

FAO studies suggest there is still scope for expanding irrigation to meet future needs. However, irrigation potential is difficult to estimate accurately, since it depends on complex data on soils, rainfall and terrain. The figures should therefore be taken only as a rough guide. The total irrigation potential in developing countries is nevertheless estimated at some 402 million ha. Of this around half was in use in 1997-99, leaving an unused potential of 200 million ha. The projected increase by 2030 would take up only 20 percent of this unused potential.

In some regions, however, irrigation will come much closer to its full potential: by 2030, East Asia and the Near East and North Africa will be using three-quarters of their irrigable area, and South Asia (excluding India) almost 90 percent.

Is there enough water?

Another frequently voiced concern is that much of the world is heading for water shortages. Since agriculture is responsible for about 70 percent of all the water withdrawn for human use, it is feared that this will affect the future of food production. Once again, at global level there seems to be no cause for alarm, but at the level of some localities, countries and regions, serious water shortages appear highly likely to arise.

The assessment of potential irrigated land used for this report already takes into account the limitations imposed by the availability of water. The renewable water resources available in a given area consist of the amount added by rainfall and incoming river flow, minus the amount lost through evapotranspiration. This may vary greatly across regions. For example, in an arid region such as the Near East and North Africa, only 18 percent of rainfall and incoming flows remain after evapotranspiration, whereas in humid East Asia the share is as high as 50 percent.

The water used for irrigation includes, besides that actually transpired by the growing crop, all the water applied to it, which may be considerable in the case of crops that are flooded, such as rice. In addition, there are the losses through leakage and evaporation on the way to the fields, and the water that drains away from the fields without being used by the crop. The ratio between the amount of water actually used for crop growth and the amount withdrawn from water sources is known as water use efficiency.

There are large regional differences in water use efficiency. Generally, efficiency is higher

The projections for developing countries imply a 14 percent increase in water withdrawals for irrigation by 2030. One in five developing countries will face water shortages.

where water availability is lower: in Latin America, for example, it is only 25 percent, compared with 40 percent in the Near East and North Africa and 44 percent in South Asia.

In the developing countries as a whole, only about 7 percent of renewable water resources were withdrawn for irrigation in 1997-99. But because of differences in efficiency and in water availability, some regions were using a much higher proportion than others. In sub-Saharan Africa, where irrigation is less widespread, only 2 percent were used, and in water-rich Latin America a mere 1 percent. In contrast, the figure in South Asia was 36 percent and in the Near East and North Africa no less than 53 percent.

The projections for developing countries imply a 14 percent increase in water withdrawals for irrigation by 2030. Even then, they will be using only 8 percent of their renewable water resources for irrigation. The shares in sub-Saharan Africa and Latin America will remain very small.

Water availability is considered to become a critical issue only when 40 percent or more of

Irrigation and water resources, 1997-99 to 2030

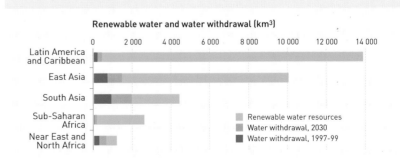

Renewable water and water withdrawal (km³)

Latin America and Caribbean
East Asia
South Asia
Sub-Saharan Africa
Near East and North Africa

■ Renewable water resources
■ Water withdrawal, 2030
■ Water withdrawal, 1997-99

Source: FAO data and projections

renewable water resources are used for irrigation. This is the level at which countries are forced to make difficult choices between their agricultural and their urban water supply sectors. By 2030 South Asia will be using this level, and the Near East and North Africa no less than 58 percent.

Out of 93 developing countries studied for this report, 10 were already using more than 40 percent in 1997-99 and another 8 were using more than 20 percent — a threshold which can be considered to indicate impending water scarcity. By 2030 two more countries will have crossed this lower threshold and one in five developing countries will be suffering actual or impending water scarcity.

Two countries, Libyan Arab Jamahiriya and Saudi Arabia, are already using more water for irrigation than their annual renewable resources, by drawing on fossil groundwater reserves. Groundwater mining also occurs at local levels in several other countries of the Near East and North Africa, South Asia and East Asia. In large areas of India and China, ground-water levels are falling by 1 to 3 metres per year, causing subsidence in buildings, intrusion of seawater into aquifers and higher pumping costs.

In these countries and areas, policy changes and investments will be needed to improve the efficiency of water use, together with innovations to improve the capture and infiltration of water, such as water harvesting, tree planting and so on.

Potential for yield growth

Growth rates have slowed in the past decade
Most future increases in crop production will be achieved through improved yields. Yield advances have been uneven over the past three decades.

Global cereal yields grew rapidly between 1961 and 1999, averaging 2.1 percent a year. Thanks to the green revolution, they grew even faster in developing countries, at an average rate of 2.5 percent a year. The fastest growth rates

Growth in wheat and rice yields slowed markedly in the 1990s. Rice yields rose at an average of 2.3 percent per year between 1961 and 1989, but between 1989 and 1999 this figure fell by more than half, to 1.1 percent.

were achieved for wheat, rice and maize which, as the world's most important food staples, have been the major focus of international breeding efforts. Yields of the major cash crops, soybean and cotton, also grew rapidly.

At the other end of the scale, yields of millet, sorghum and pulses saw only slow growth. These crops, grown mainly by resource-poor farmers in semi-arid areas, are ones for which international research has not so far come up with varieties that deliver large yield gains under farm conditions. There have been useful incremental gains, however, and farmers' yields are more stable than they used to be, thanks to the introduction of traits such as early maturity.

Overall growth in cereal yields slowed in the 1990s. Maize yields in developing countries maintained their upward momentum, but gains in wheat and rice slowed markedly. Wheat yields grew at an average of 3.8 percent per year between 1961 and 1989, but at only 2 percent a year in 1989 to 1999. For rice the respective rates fell by more than half, from 2.3 percent to 1.1 percent. This largely reflects the slower growth in demand for these products.

Is projected yield growth realistic?
The slower growth in production projected for the next 30 years means that yields will not need to grow as rapidly as in the past. Growth in wheat yields is projected to slow to 1.1 percent a year in the next 30 years, while rice yields are expected to rise by only 0.9 percent per year.

Nevertheless, increased yields will be required — so is the projected increase feasible? One way of judging is to look at the difference in performance between groups of countries. Some developing countries have attained very high crop yields. In 1997-99, for example, the top performing 10 percent had average wheat yields more than six times higher that those of the worst performing 10 percent and twice as high as the average in the largest producers, China, India and Turkey. For rice the gaps were roughly similar.

National yield differences like these are due to two main sets of causes:

• Some of the differences are due to differing conditions of soil, climate and slope. In Mexico, for example, much of the country is arid or semi-arid and less than a fifth of the land cultivated to maize is suitable for improved hybrid varieties. As a result, the country's maize yield of 2.4 tonnes per ha is not much more than a quarter of the United States average. Yield gaps of this kind, caused by agro-ecological differences, cannot be narrowed.

• Other parts of the yield gap, however, are the result of differences in crop management practices, such as the amount of fertilizer used. These gaps can be narrowed, if it is economic for farmers to do so.

To find out what progress in yields is feasible, it is necessary to distinguish between the gaps that can be narrowed and those that cannot. A detailed FAO/IIASA study based on agro-ecological zones has taken stock of the amount of land in each country that is suitable, in varying degrees, for different crops. Using these data it is possible to work out a national maximum obtainable yield for each crop.

This maximum assumes that high levels of inputs and the best suited crop varieties are used for each area, and that each crop is grown on a range of land quality that reflects the national mix. It is a realistic figure because it is based on technologies already known and does not assume any major breakthroughs in plant breeding. If anything, it is likely to under-estimate maximum obtainable yields, because in practice crops will tend to be grown on the land best suited for them.

The maximum obtainable yield can then be compared with actual national average yield to

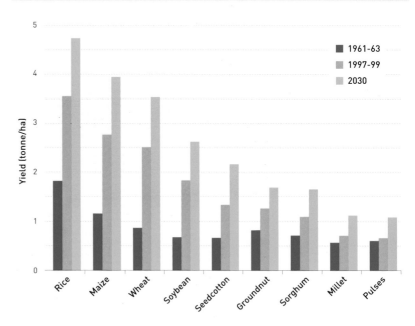

Crop yields in developing countries, 1961 to 2030

- ■ 1961-63
- ■ 1997-99
- ■ 2030

Yield (tonne/ha)

Rice　Maize　Wheat　Soybean　Seedcotton　Groundnut　Sorghum　Millet　Pulses

Source: FAO data and projections

give some idea of the yield gap that can be bridged. The study showed that even a techno-logically progressive country such as France is not yet close to reaching its maximum obtainable yield. France could obtain an average wheat yield of 8.7 tonnes per ha, rising to 11.6 tonnes per ha on her best wheat land, yet her actual average yield today is only 7.2 tonnes per ha.

Similar yield gaps exist for most countries studied in this way. Only a few countries are

The slower growth in production projected for the next 30 years means that yields will not need to grow as rapidly as in the past. Growth in wheat yields is projected to slow to 1.1 percent and in rice yields to only 0.9 percent per year in developing countries.

Exploitable yield gaps for wheat: actual versus obtainable yield

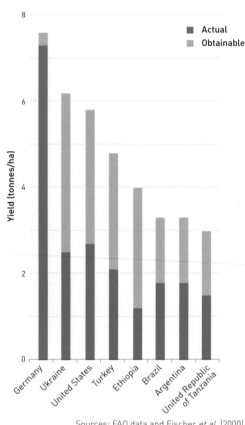

Sources: FAO data and Fischer et al. (2000)

Fertilizer use, 1961 to 1999

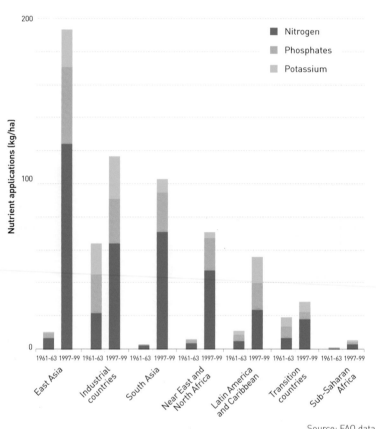

Source: FAO data

actually achieving their maximum obtainable yield.

When real prices rise, there is every reason to believe that farmers will work to bridge yield gaps. In the past, farmers with good access to technologies, inputs and markets have responded very quickly to higher prices. Argentina, for example, increased her wheat production by no less than 68 percent in just one year (1996), following price rises, although this was done mainly be extending the area under wheat. Where land is scarcer, farmers respond by switching to higher-yielding varieties and increasing their use of other inputs to achieve higher yields.

It seems clear that, even if no more new technologies become available, there is still scope for increasing crop yields in line with requirements. Indeed, if just 11 of the countries that produce wheat, accounting for less than two-fifths of world production, were to bridge only half the gap between their maximum obtainable and their actual yields, then the world's wheat output would increase by almost a quarter.

The outcome of research is always uncertain, particularly if it is strategic or basic in nature. However, if new technologies do become available through the genetic and other research currently under way, this could raise yield ceilings still further, while possibly also reducing the environmental costs of crop production.

Given the right economic incentives, world agriculture will respond to the demand expressed in the marketplace, as it has done in the past. Of course, many poor farmers in marginal environments will be in a position to respond only if they gain access to inputs, markets and technologies, and if the policy environment is favourable. In addition, research must develop the varieties and techniques needed to raise yields in difficult environments. These measures are essential if poor farmers and their families are not to find themselves trapped in poverty.

Fertilizer: use will continue to rise, but slowly

One of the major ways in which farmers can increase yields is by applying more fertilizer. A third of the increase in world cereal production in the 1970s and 1980s has been attributed to increased fertilizer use. In India this figure rises to half.

The level of fertilizer use varies enormously between regions. North America, Western Europe and East and South Asia accounted for four-fifths of world fertilizer use in 1997-99. The highest rates, averaging 194 kg of nutrients per ha, were applied in East Asia, followed by the industrial countries with 117 kg per ha. At the other end of the scale, farmers in sub-Saharan Africa applied a mere 5 kg per ha.

World fertilizer consumption grew rapidly in the 1960s, 1970s and 1980s, but slowed considerably in the 1990s. The slowdown in industrial countries was due mainly to reduced government support for agriculture and increased concern over the environmental impact. In transition countries, fertilizer consumption also fell rapidly, but for different reasons, namely recession and restructuring. Even in developing countries, the growth rate of fertilizer use in the 1990s was less than half of that seen in earlier decades.

This slower growth is projected to continue. Global fertilizer consumption is expected to grow by an average 1 percent per year over the next three decades (a little faster in developing countries and a little slower in developed). The fastest growth rates are expected in sub-Saharan Africa. Here fertilizer use is currently very low, so fast growth rates can still mean only small absolute increases.

The role of technology

The development and dissemination of new technology is an important factor determining the future of agriculture. The FAO study investigated three areas that are particularly critical, namely biotechnology, technologies in support of sustainable agriculture, and the directions that should be taken by future research.

Biotechnology: issues and prospects

What is the current role of biotechnology?
For thousands of years, human beings have been engaged in improving the crops and animals they raise. Over the past 150 years,

Biotechnology promises great benefits for both producers and consumers of agricultural products, but its applications are also associated with potential risks. The risks and benefits may vary substantially from one product to the next and are often perceived differently in different countries. To reap the full potential of biotechnology, appropriate policies must be developed to ensure that the potential risks are accurately diagnosed and, where necessary, avoided.

scientists have assisted their efforts by developing and refining the techniques of selection and breeding. Though considerable progress has been achieved, conventional selection and breeding are time-consuming and bear technical limitations.

Modern biotechnology has the potential to speed up the development and deployment of improved crops and animals. Marker-assisted selection, for instance, increases the efficiency of conventional plant breeding by allowing rapid, laboratory-based analysis of thousands of

individuals without the need to grow plants to maturity in the field. The techniques of tissue culture allow the rapid multiplication of clean planting materials of vegetatively propagated species for distribution to farmers. Genetic engineering or modification — manipulating an organism's genome by introducing or eliminating specific genes — helps transfer desired traits between plants more quickly and accurately than is possible in conventional breeding.

This latter technique promises considerable benefits but has also aroused widespread public concerns. These include ethical misgivings, anxieties about food and environmental safety, and fears about the concentration of economic power and technological dependence, which could deepen the technological divide between developed and developing countries.

The spread of genetically modified (GM) crops has been rapid. Their area increased by a factor of 30 over the 5 years to 2001, when they covered more than 52 million ha. Considerable research to develop more GM varieties is under way in some developing countries. China, for instance, is reported to have the second largest biotechnology research capacity after the United States.

However, the spread so far is geographically very limited. Just four countries account for 99 percent of the global GM crop area: the United States with 35.7 million ha, Argentina with 11.8 million ha, Canada with 3.2 million ha

Area of GM crops for different commodities and countries

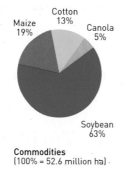

Maize 19%
Cotton 13%
Canola 5%
Soybean 63%

Commodities
(100% = 52.6 million ha)

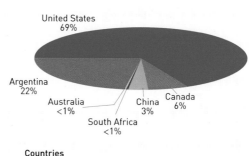

United States 69%
Argentina 22%
Australia <1%
China 3%
Canada 6%
South Africa <1%

Countries
(100% = 52.6 million ha)

Source: ISAAA (2001)

and China with 1.5 million ha. The number and type of crops and applications involved is also limited: two-thirds of the GM area is planted to herbicide-tolerant crops. All commercially

Biotechnology: potential benefits, risks and concerns

Potential benefits

- Increased productivity, leading to higher incomes for producers and lower prices for consumers.
- Less need for environmentally harmful inputs, particularly insecticides. Scientists have developed maize and cotton varieties incorporating genes from the bacterium *Bacillus thuringensis* (Bt) which produce insecticidal toxins. Virus- and fungus-resistant varieties are in the pipeline for fruits and vegetables, potato and wheat.
- New crop varieties for marginal areas, increasing the sustainability of agriculture in poor farming communities. These varieties will be resistant to drought, waterlogging, soil acidity, salinity or extreme temperatures.
- Reduced dependence on management skills through built-in resistance to pests and diseases.
- Enhanced food security through reduced fluctuations in yields caused by insect invasions, droughts or floods.
- Higher nutritional values through higher protein quality and content as well as increased levels of vitamins and micro-nutrients (e.g. iodine or beta-carotene enriched rice).
- Better health value and digestibility. Scientists are developing varieties of soybean that contain less saturated fat and more sucrose.
- Production of valuable chemicals and pharmaceuticals at lower cost than is possible at present. Products envisaged range from speciality oils and biodegradable plastics to hormones and human antibodies.

Risks and concerns

- Products are tailored largely to the needs of large-scale farmers and industrial process-ing in the developed world, with the result that resource-poor farmers in developing countries will fail to benefit.
- Market concentration and monopoly power in the seed industry, reducing choice and control for farmers, who will pay ever higher prices for seed. One company alone controls over 80 percent of the market for GM cotton and 33 percent for GM soybean.
- Patenting of genes and other materials originating in the developing countries. Private-sector companies are able to appropriate without compensation the products resulting from the breeding efforts of generations of farmers and from research conducted in the public sector.
- Technologies that prevent farmers re-using seed. These require farmers to purchase seed afresh every season and could inhibit adoption by poor farmers. In the worst case, ignorance of this characteristic could result in complete crop failure.
- Food safety. This has received added attention after a potentially allergenic maize variety that was not registered for food use entered the food chain in the United States.
- The environmental impact of GM crops. There is a risk that inserted genes may spread to wild populations, with potentially serious consequences for biodiversity, or contaminate the crops of organic farmers. Genes for herbicide resistance could encourage the overuse of herbicides, while those for insect resistance could generate resistance in insects, forcing the use of more toxic products to kill them.

grown GM crops are currently either non-food crops (cotton) or are heavily used in animal feeds (soybean and maize).

Why do we need modern biotechnology?

Globally, agricultural production could probably meet expected demand over the period to 2030 even without major advances in biotechnology. However, biotechnology could be a major tool in the fight against hunger and poverty, especially in developing countries. Because it may deliver solutions where conventional breeding approaches have failed, it could greatly assist the development of crop varieties able to thrive in the difficult environments where many of the world's poor live and farm. Some promising results have already been achieved in the development of varieties with complex traits such as resistance or tolerance to drought, soil salinity, insect pests and diseases, helping to reduce crop failures. Several applications allow resource-poor farmers to reduce their use of purchased inputs such as pesticides or fertilizers, with benefits to the environment and human health as well as farmers' incomes.

Most biotechnology is generated and controlled by large private-sector companies, which have so far mainly targeted the commercial farmers who can afford their products. Nevertheless, there is some public-sector work directed towards the needs of resource-poor farmers. In addition, most of the technologies and intermediate products developed through private-sector research could be adapted to solve priority problems in the developing countries. If the poor of these countries are to reap this potential, national and international action is needed to foster private-public partnerships that will promote access to these technologies at affordable prices. This is the main policy challenge for the future.

What policies are needed to harness the potential of biotechnology for the poor?

In the case of GM crops, most of the commercial applications developed so far are directed towards reducing production costs, not towards meeting the needs expressed by consumers. The perception of the expected benefits and

Bt cotton in China: a success story

One of the most impressive successes in agricultural biotechnology is China's experience with Bt cotton.

Following research by various public- and private-sector partners, Bt cotton was released to the country's farmers in 1997. It quickly became very popular, with the area devoted to it expanding from 2000 ha in the first year to 70 000 ha in 2000. The reasons for this popularity were mainly economic, but there were important environmental and human health benefits too.

In general, cotton is very susceptible to pests and normally requires many applications of insecticide, which are expensive, require a great deal of extra labour, and often cause health problems in farm workers. Farmers using the new Bt variety needed over 80 percent less insecticide than those using non-Bt varieties and only a third as many applications. They were able to cut both their labour and other input costs. Their yields were also higher: 3.37 tonnes per ha as opposed to 3.18 tonnes with non-Bt cotton. The overall cost of producing a kilogramme of cotton was 28 percent lower.

There were positive effects on biodiversity, with farmers and government extension agents reporting a greater variety of insects and more beneficial species in fields with Bt cotton. In addition there were considerable health benefits for the farmers: only 5 percent of Bt cotton growers reported poisonings, against 22 per cent of growers of non-Bt cotton. The overall economic benefits of Bt cotton were assessed at US$334 million per year in 1999.

potential risks of such crops, and of biotechnology as a whole, differ among regions, countries, interest groups and individuals. The urban and landless poor in developing countries need

Effects of Bt cotton in China

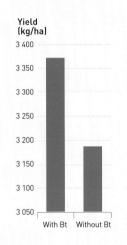

Yield
(kg/ha)

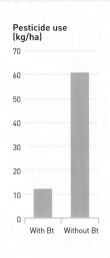

Pesticide use
(kg/ha)

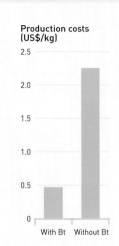

Production costs
(US$/kg)

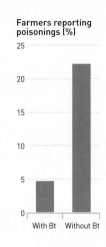

Farmers reporting
poisonings (%)

Source: Huang *et al.* (2002)

cheaper food. In contrast, for consumers in developed countries, where food is plentiful, the health and environmental concerns associated with biotechnology outweigh the possible cost savings. These consumers will be more inclined to accept the new products if they can be assured of their safety through appropriate regulatory frameworks.

Greater and better targeted investments in GM research for developing countries will be needed to ensure that the farmers of these countries have access to the resulting new crop varieties. The focus should shift from pesticide-tolerant crops towards the characteristics that matter to resource-poor farmers: improved resistance or tolerance to drought, waterlogging, salinity and extreme temperatures; improved resistance to pests and diseases; better nutritional values; and higher yields. Such a shift could be based on new private-public partnerships, exploiting the greater efficiency of private-sector research but under the guidance of public-sector donors. Research funds could be made available on the basis of public tenders.

Further change is on the horizon

The rapid progress made in both generating and extending new biotechnology applications,

together with the uncertain public response to these applications, make it difficult to predict the long-term prospects for these technologies, including their impact on future production. However, developments in the short term — the next 3 years or so — are somewhat easier to foresee.

The success of Bt cotton in China has paved the way for further expansion of GM crops in this country, which has considerable potential for GM products. China is a major producer of soybean, maize and tobacco — all crops for which GM traits have been developed elsewhere. Wide-scale adoption of GM technology in China could well provide the impetus for other developing countries to follow suit.

While the adoption rates for GM technologies in developing countries are likely to rise, they are expected to slow in the developed world. This mainly reflects the impressive growth of the past, which limits the remaining potential. GM soybean, for instance, already accounts for two-thirds of the soybean area worldwide and for an even larger share of the area in developed countries. As the global area of such crops expands, other, more sophisticated biotechnology applications may gain importance. Examples include GM-based nutraceuticals or cosmetic applications. As these new applications are likely to produce a broader range of benefits than "merely" cheaper foods and feeds, consumers in the developed countries may become more inclined to accept them.

Towards sustainable agriculture

Given a conducive policy environment, the next three decades should see the spread of farming methods that reduce environmental damage while maintaining or even increasing production. In some cases these technologies will also reduce the costs of production.

The negative impact that soil tillage can have on soil biological processes and hence on productivity has been increasingly recognized. In response, no-till or conservation agriculture (NT/CA) has been developed. This form of agriculture can maintain and improve crop yields, providing greater resilience against drought and other stresses.

Like organic farming, NT/CA sustains biodiversity and saves on the use of resources. However, unlike organic farming, it can be combined with synthetic inputs and GM crops. It involves three principal elements:

- Minimal disturbance of the soil. No tillage occurs and crops are planted directly through the soil cover. Besides reducing the loss of nutrients to the atmosphere, this sustains soil structure and ecology.
- Maintenance of a permanent cover of live or dead plant material. This protects the soil against erosion and compaction by rain and inhibits the growth of weeds.
- Crop rotation. Different crops are planted over several seasons so as to avoid the buildup of

pests and diseases and to optimize the use of nutrients.

NT/CA can raise crop yields by 20 to 50 percent. Yields are less variable from year to year, while labour and fuel costs are lower. Once demonstrated to farmers at a given location, NT/CA tends to spread spontaneously over a larger area. The main obstacles to its spread are the complexity of managing crop rotation, the transitional costs of switching to new practices and, to a certain extent, the conservatism of agricultural extension services. Retraining, sometimes combined with increased financial incentives, may be needed to speed the pace of adoption.

Integrated pest management
Pesticides involve a range of hazards in their production, distribution and application. When used conventionally, they can eliminate natural predators as well as target pests, and generate resistance in pests. They may also pollute water and soil resources and cause a range of health problems to operators and their families.

Integrated pest management (IPM) aims to minimize the amount of pesticides applied by using other control methods more effectively. Pest incidence is monitored, and action is taken only when damage exceeds tolerable limits. The other technologies and methods used include pest-resistant varieties, bio-insecticides and traps, and the management of crop rotations, fertilizer use and irrigation in such a way as to minimize pests. Chemical pesticides, if they are used at all, are chosen for minimum toxicity and applied in carefully calculated ways.

Many countries have successfully introduced IPM and have experienced increased production accompanied by lower financial, environmental and human health costs as a result. Again, extension systems and policy frameworks in many countries have tended to favour the use of pesticides. These must be reformed if IPM is to spread faster in future.

Integrated plant nutrient systems
All crop production uses up plant nutrients in the soil. Conventional fertilizers usually replace only a few key nutrients, while others continue

No-till/conservation agriculture can raise crop yields by 20 to 50 percent. Yields are more stable, resilience against drought improves and labour and fuel costs are lower, but management is more complex.

to be depleted. Many resource-poor farmers cannot afford these fertilizers, resulting in soil mining. In other cases there is overuse, leading to the pollution of soils and water resources.

An integrated plant nutrient system is one in which practitioners aim to optimize the use of nutrients through a range of practices that include the recycling of vegetable and animal wastes and the use of legumes to fix atmospheric nitrogen. External nutrients are used judiciously, in ways that minimize costs and reduce pollution. Managing the use of fertilizers precisely can increase their efficiency by 10 to 30 percent.

The promise of organic agriculture

Organic agriculture is a set of practices in which the use of external inputs is minimized. Synthetic pesticides, chemical fertilizers, synthetic preservatives, pharmaceuticals, GM organisms, sewage sludge and irradiation are all excluded.

Interest in organic agriculture has been boosted by public concerns over pollution, food safety and human and animal health, as well as by the value set on nature and the country-side. Consumers in developed countries have shown themselves willing to pay price premiums of 10 to 40 percent for organic produce, while government subsidies have helped to make organic agriculture economically viable.

As a result, organic agriculture has expanded rapidly in Western countries. Between 1995 and 2000, the total area of organic land in Europe and the United States tripled, albeit from a very low base.

In 2001, some 15.8 million ha were under certified organic agriculture globally. Almost

half of this was in Oceania, just under a quarter in Europe and a fifth in Latin America. About two-thirds of the area is organic grassland. As a percentage of total agricultural land, organic agriculture is still modest — an average of 2 percent in Europe. However, many European countries have ambitious targets for expansion, with the result that Western Europe may have around a quarter of its total agricultural land under organic management by 2030.

With a number of large supermarket chains now involved, the market for organic foods is booming and potential demand far outstrips supply. In many industrial countries, sales are growing at 15 to 30 percent a year. The total market in 2000 was estimated at almost US$20 billion — still less than 2 percent of total retail food sales in industrial countries but a sizeable increase over the value a decade ago.

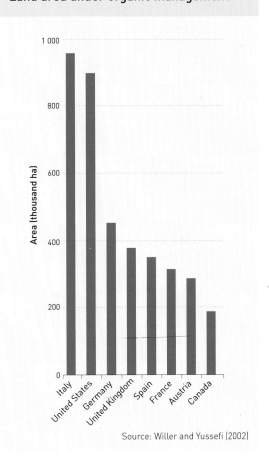

Land area under organic management

Source: Willer and Yussefi (2002)

Demand is expected to continue to grow, perhaps even faster than the 20 percent or so achieved in recent years. The supply shortfall offers opportunities for developing countries to fill the gap, especially with out-of-season produce.

In industrial countries, organic agriculture is based on clearly defined methods enforced by inspection and certification bodies. Most developing countries, in contrast, do not yet have their own organic standards and certification systems. In these countries, organic agriculture may in fact be more wide-spread than in the developed world but is practised of necessity, since the majority of farmers are unable to afford or cannot obtain modern inputs. Most organic crops for local consumption are sold at the same price as other produce. However, many developing countries are now producing organic commodities in commercial quantities for export to developed country markets. These exports can be expected to increase in the coming years.

Organic agriculture offers many environmental benefits. Agrochemicals can pollute groundwater, disrupt key ecological processes such as pollination, harm beneficial micro-organisms and cause health hazards to farm workers. Modern monoculture using synthetic inputs often harms biodiversity at the genetic, species and ecosystem levels. The external costs of conventional agriculture can be substantial.

In contrast, organic agriculture sets out to enhance biodiversity and restore the natural ecological balance. It encourages both spatial and temporal biodiversity through intercropping and crop rotations, conserves soil and water resources and builds soil organic matter and biological processes. Pests and diseases are kept at bay by crop associations, symbiotic combinations and other non-chemical methods. Water pollution is reduced or eliminated.

Although yields are often 10 to 30 percent lower than in conventional farming, organic agriculture can give excellent profits. In industrial countries, consumer premiums, government subsidies and agritourism boost incomes from organic farms. In developing countries, well-designed organic systems can give better yields, profits and returns on labour than traditional systems. In Madagascar, hundreds of farmers have found they can increase their rice yields fourfold, to as much as 8 tonnes per ha, by using improved organic management practices. In the Philippines, organic rice yields of over 6 tonnes per ha have been recorded. Experiences of organic production in low-potential areas such as Northern Potosí (Bolivia), Wardha (India) and Kitale (Kenya) have shown that yields can be doubled or tripled over those obtained using traditional practices.

Organic agriculture also has social benefits. It uses cheap, locally available materials and usually requires more labour, thereby increasing employment opportunities. This is a considerable advantage in areas where, or at times when, there is a labour surplus. By rehabilitating traditional practices and foods, organic agriculture can promote social cohesion.

Certain policy measures are essential if the progress of organic agriculture is to continue. Support for agriculture is increasingly shifting from production goals to environmental and social goals, a trend that could favour organic agriculture. Agreed international standards and accreditation are needed to remove obstacles to trade. Extensionists often promote the idea that synthetic inputs are best and may need training in organic methods. Research to solve technical problems needs to be stepped up. Secure land tenure is essential if farmers are to undertake the long process of conversion to organic standards. If these measures are put in place, organic agriculture could become a realistic alternative to traditional agriculture over the next 30 years, at least at the local level.

Locally, organic agriculture could become a realistic alternative to traditional agriculture over the next 30 years.

Directions for research

Strengths and weaknesses of past research

The green revolution has played a key role in the major improvements in food supply over the past 40 years. The yields of rice, wheat and maize in developing countries have risen by 100 to 200 percent since the late 1960s.

Yield gains were the primary focus of the green revolution. Breeding and selection led to the development of improved crop varieties, but greatly increased use of inputs, such as fertilizer, pesticides and irrigation water, were needed to get the best out of these varieties. The green revolution achieved its aims not just through research but through a package of methods and inputs pushed by national and international agencies, extension services and private-sector companies.

But this first green revolution had its shortcomings:

- It was heavily geared to the world's three leading cereal crops, which were suited to its emphasis on maximizing yields. Other crops, including many that are important in sub-Saharan African, such as cassava, millet, sorghum, banana, groundnut and sweet potato, needed a different approach.
- It was suited only to areas with good soils and water supplies, and largely neglected the more marginal rainfed areas with problem soils and uncertain rainfall.
- It relied on farmers being able to afford inputs, and did little for poor smallholders with insufficient funds or access to credit.
- Finally, it largely ignored the possible environmental consequences of high input use, such as the pollution of water and soils with nitrates and pesticides.

Needed: a doubly green revolution

A second, doubly green revolution is now needed. Its goals, as with the first, must include increased productivity. But it must also aim for sustainability — minimizing or reducing the environmental impacts of agriculture — and for equity — making sure that the benefits of research spread to the poor and to marginal areas.

Productivity must increase on all the lands where farmers seek a living, not just in the well-endowed areas. More varieties and packages for crops other than the three key cereals need to be developed. And the potential of resource-conserving approaches such as IPM needs to be fully realized.

Research for the new green revolution needs to be genuinely multidisciplinary. It must cover not only the biological sciences, including genetic engineering alongside conventional breeding and agronomy, but also the socio-economic context in which farming occurs. And it must focus not only on crops and animals but on the ecology of all life forms within the farming system. Areas of special importance in ecology include the interactions of plants, pests and predators, and competition between crops and weeds. Plant rooting systems and the availability of nutrients and soil organic matter also deserve more emphasis.

Above all, priority must be given to the needs of the poor in the marginal, rainfed areas bypassed by the first green revolution. Scientists must engage in an interactive dialogue with all the stakeholders in the research process, especially farmers but also policy makers, civic society and the general public.

Research towards this second green revolution is already under way in some locations. Its first fruits have shown that it can be successful,

Key questions for researchers:

- Will the technology lead to higher productivity across all farms, soil types and regions, not just well-endowed ones?
- How will the technology affect the seasonal and annual stability of production?
- How will the technology affect the ecosystem and the sustainability of farming?
- Who will be the winners and losers from the technology — and how will it affect the poor?

especially when farmers participate actively in the design and testing of new technology. However, the research effort needs to be greatly strengthened and the challenge of scaling up the results of research has yet to be adequately addressed.

Livestock: intensification and its risks

Meat and dairy products will provide an increasing share of the human diet, with poultry expanding fastest. Future demand can be met, but the negative environmental consequences of increased production must be addressed.

Livestock production currently accounts for some 40 percent of the gross value of world agricultural production, and its share is rising. It is the world's largest user of agricultural land, directly as pasture and indirectly through the production of fodder crops and other feedstuffs. In 1999 some 3 460 million ha were under permanent pasture — more than twice the area under arable and permanent crops.

Livestock provide not only meat, but dairy products, eggs, wool, hides and other goods. They can be closely integrated into mixed farming systems as consumers of crop by-products and sources of organic fertilizer, while larger animals also provide power for ploughing and transport.

Livestock have a considerable impact on the environment. Growth of the livestock sector has been a major factor contributing to deforestation in some countries, particularly in Latin America. Overstocking land with grazing animals can cause soil erosion, desertification and the loss of plant biodiversity. Public health hazards are increasing with the intensification of urban and peri-urban livestock production. Wastes from industrial livestock facilities can pollute water supplies and livestock are major sources of greenhouse gases.

Diets shift from staples to meat

The past three decades have seen major shifts in human diets. The share of animal products has risen, while that of cereals and other staples has fallen. And within the meat sector there has been a dramatic rise in the share of poultry and, to a smaller extent, pig meat. These trends are likely to continue over the next 30 years, though in less dramatic form.

As incomes rise, people generally prefer to spend a higher share of their food budget on animal protein, so meat and dairy consumption tends to grow faster than that of food crops. As a result, the past three decades have seen buoyant growth in the consumption of livestock products, especially in newly industrializing countries.

Annual meat consumption per person in developing countries as a whole more than doubled between 1964-66 and 1997-99, from only 10.2 kg per year to 25.5 kg — a rise of 2.8 percent a year. The growth was much less (from 10 kg to 15.5 kg) if China and Brazil are excluded. The rise was particularly rapid for

Livestock are the world's largest user of agricultural land: in 1999 some 3 460 million ha were under permanent pasture — more than twice the area under arable and permanent crops.

poultry, where consumption per person grew more than fivefold. Pig meat consumption also rose strongly, though most of this rise was concentrated in China.

The overall rise was unevenly spread: in China meat consumption has quadrupled over the past two decades, whereas in sub-Saharan Africa it has remained stagnant, at under 10 kg per person. Differences in meat consumption between countries can be substantial because of differences in meat availability or in dietary habits, including the role of fish in the provision of total animal protein. For example, meat consumption in Mongolia is as high as 79 kg per person, but overall diets are grossly insufficient and undernourishment is widespread. Meat consumption in the United States and Japan, two countries of comparable living standards, is 120 kg and 42 kg per person respectively, but their per capita consumption of fish and seafood is 20 kg and 66 kg.

Future growth may slow

Looking towards 2030, the trend towards increased consumption of livestock products will continue in the developing countries. However, future growth in consumption of both meat and milk may not be as rapid as in the recent past, given the reduced scope for further increases in major consuming countries.

In developed countries the scope for increased demand is limited. Population growth is slow and the consumption of livestock products is already very high. At the same time health and food safety concerns, focused on animal fats and the emergence of new diseases such as bovine spongiform encephalopathy (BSE) and variant Creutzfeldt-Jakob disease (vCJD), are

holding back demand for meat. Total meat consumption in the industrial countries has risen by only 1.3 percent a year over the past ten years.

In developing countries the demand for meat has grown rapidly over the past 20 years, at 5.6 percent a year. Over the next two decades this rate is projected to slow by half. Part of this slowdown will be due to slower population growth and part to the same factor that is at work in developed countries: the countries that have dominated past increases, such as China and Brazil, have now reached fairly high levels of consumption and so have less scope for further rises. In India, which will rival China as the most populous country in the world in the 2040s, the growth of meat consumption may be limited by cultural factors in addition to the continued prevalence of low incomes, since many of India's people are likely to remain vegetarians. However, India's consumption of dairy products is projected to continue to rise rapidly, building on the successes achieved over the past 30 years. In sub-Saharan Africa, slow economic growth will limit increases in both meat and dairy consumption.

The rise in poultry consumption looks set to continue, though a little more slowly than in the

Annual meat consumption per person in developing countries more than doubled between 1964-66 and 1997-99, but there were substantial differences between countries.

World average meat consumption per person, 1964-66 to 2030

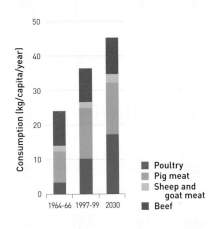

Source: FAO data and projections

past, from a global average of 10.2 kg per person in 1997-99 to 17.2 kg by 2030. Much smaller increases in world per capita consumption are foreseen for both pig meat and beef.

Bigger herds, fatter animals

Given the slower growth of demand, livestock production will also grow more slowly than in the past. Moreover, increased efficiency in the sector could mean that extra demand can be met by a smaller growth in the number of animals. In absolute terms, however, the number of animals will still need to rise considerably. The projections show an extra 360 million cattle and buffaloes, 560 million extra sheep and goats, and 190 million extra pigs by 2030 — rises of 24, 32 and 22 percent respectively.

However, it should prove possible to meet much of the extra demand by increasing productivity rather than animal numbers. There is ample scope for this in developing countries, particularly with regard to cattle productivity. In 1997-99 the yield of beef per animal in developing countries was 163 kg compared with 284 kg in industrialized countries, while average milk yields were 1.1 and 5.9 tonnes per year per cow respectively.

Selection and breeding, together with improved feeding regimes, could lead to faster fattening and larger animals. The average carcass weight for cattle, for example, has already risen from 174 kg in 1967-69 to 198 kg 30 years later; by 2030 it could reach 211 kg. The offtake rate should also rise, as animals will be ready for market earlier.

The shift to more intensive production will continue

A continued shift in production methods can be expected, away from extensive grazing systems and towards more intensive and industrial methods.

Grazing on pasture still provides 30 percent of total beef production, but its market share is declining. In South and Central America, grazing is often pursued on land cleared from rainforests, where it fuels soil degradation and further deforestation. In semi-arid environments, overstocking during dry periods frequently brings risks of desertification, although it has been shown that pastures do recover quickly if stock are taken off and good rains return.

Mixed farming, in which livestock provide manure and draught power in addition to milk and meat, still predominates for cattle. As populations and economies grow, these multi-purpose types of farming will tend to give way to more specialized enterprises.

> In recent years, livestock production from industrial enterprises has grown twice as fast as that from more traditional mixed farming systems and more than six times faster than from grazing systems.

Where land is scarce, more intensive systems of stall-feeding emerge. In these systems, fodder is cut and brought to the stabled animals, leading to less soil damage and faster fattening. This trend too can be expected to continue and accelerate.

More industrial and commercial forms of production will gradually increase in both number and scale. These intensive enterprises will make use of improved genetic material, sophisticated feeding systems, animal health prophylactics and highly skilled management. In recent years, industrial livestock production has grown at twice the rate of more traditional mixed farming systems and at more than six times the rate of production based on grazing. At the turn of the century industrial enterprises accounted for 74 percent of the world's total poultry production, 68 percent of its eggs and 40 percent of its pig meat.

Current trends towards industrial and commercial production could pose a threat to the estimated 675 million rural poor whose livelihoods depend on livestock. Without special measures, the poor will find it harder to compete and may become marginalized, descending into still deeper poverty. Yet, if the policy environment is right, the future growth in demand for livestock products could provide an opportunity for poor families to generate additional income and employment. Because of its low capital costs, and its ability to make use of wastes and communally owned resources, livestock production allows poor families to accumulate assets and diversify risks, besides serving as a valuable source of products that improve both cash income and family nutrition. Policy measures that will help the poor enter and stay in the expanding market for livestock products include the provision of low-cost credit, technical support — especially in animal health and quality matters — and better access to markets through improved infrastructure and institutions.

The growing demand for livestock products offers an opportunity for the 675 million rural poor who depend on livestock to improve their livelihoods.

Environment and health problems

Commercial and industrial systems bring their own environmental problems, which differ from those of extensive systems. The concentration of animals, particularly in urban areas, leads to problems of waste disposal and pollution. Higher animal densities and transport to more distant markets often involve the frustration of natural animal behaviour, bringing distress. Increased trade in livestock products and feedstuffs brings greater risk of disease transmission, both within and across national boundaries. This applies both to diseases limited to livestock, such as foot-and-mouth, and to those that may affect both livestock and humans, such as avian flu.

Infectious animal diseases such as rinderpest or foot-and-mouth are still major threats in developing countries. Increased trade can spread them more widely, even to developed countries. Eradication programmes are shifting away from countrywide control strategies towards more focused and flexible approaches, with the aim of improving the cost-effectiveness of control.

In humid and subhumid Africa, trypanosomiasis (sleeping sickness) poses an enormous obstacle to human health and cattle production. Trypanocidal drugs, aerial spraying, adhesive insecticides, impregnated screens and traps and the use of sterile insects offer the promise of recovering infested areas for mixed farming. This will improve human health and nutrition, as well as livestock and crop production.

Industrial livestock enterprises use antibiotics on a large scale. This practice has contributed to antibiotic resistance among bacteria, including those that cause human diseases. Resistance to antihelminthics is emerging among livestock parasites. Industrial enterprises also use growth hormones to speed fattening and increase the efficiency of conversion of feed into meat. Public concern has led to restrictions on use in the EU, although negative impacts on human health have not been proved.

Increased trade in livestock products and feedstuffs brings greater risk of disease transmission, both within and across national boundaries.

Promises and risks of biotechnology

Biotechnology will have a profound effect on the future of livestock production. Some biotechnology applications are already in use, while others are still under research.

Artificial insemination, already routine in developed countries, will spread in developing countries. It can greatly increase the efficiency of animal breeding.

61

The cloning of mammalian cells could also boost productivity and output, particularly for dairy cattle in developed countries. However, the problems with this technology must be solved: currently only 2 to 5 percent of attempts to clone animals actually succeed, and cloned animals often develop serious health problems.

Rapid advances in understanding the genetic make-up of animals will provide additional potential for productivity growth. Genes that are important for economic performance, such as those for disease resistance or for adaptation to adverse environmental conditions, can be identified and transferred into more productive backgrounds, either through marker-assisted selection or through GM. These applications could prove especially useful in developing countries.

GM animals have so far been used mainly for biomedical research or the production of human proteins. GM cattle, sheep, pigs and chickens are now being produced experimentally, with the intention of eventual use for human consumption. Despite signs of consumer resistance to GM foods for direct human consumption, products from livestock fed with GM maize, soybean and cottonseed cake are already on the market.

The main risks of genetic modification arise from potential side-effects on the environment or on human health. These risks are particularly pronounced if there is insufficient testing before widespread release. There is also the risk of narrowing the genetic base and concentrating its control in the hands of large multinational corporations. Almost 5 000 breeds and strains of farm animals have been identified. Some 600 of these face extinction and many more may be at risk if the genetic resource base is not conserved.

Cereals used as feed: threat or safety valve?

Globally, some 660 million tonnes of cereals are used as livestock feed each year. This represents just over a third of total world cereal use.

This use of cereals is often perceived as a threat to food security, since it appears to remove from the market supplies of essential foods that would otherwise be available to poor countries and families, thereby raising food prices. However, it is important to realize that if these cereals were not used as feed, they would probably not be produced at all, so would not be available as food in any case.

The use of cereals as feed may actually help food security. The commercial livestock sector is responsive to the price of cereals: whenever shortages raise prices, livestock producers tend to switch to other feeds, releasing more cereals for food use. As a result, the food use of cereals may contract less than it would have done otherwise. In short, the use of cereals as feed serves as a buffer, protecting food intakes from supply variations.

In recent years the use of cereals as feeds has declined in relative terms. One reason is the growing use of cereal substitutes in livestock feed rations. Another is the collapse of the livestock sector in the transition countries, which led to reduced demand for feed in these countries. A third factor is the shift of meat production to poultry, which are much more efficient converters of feed than other livestock species.

Over the next three decades growth in the use of cereals as feeds is projected to be higher than in the recent past, accounting for half the additional use of cereals. This is partly because the transition countries will resume their agricultural growth and partly because the shift into poultry is expected to be slower.

India's white revolution

Launched in 1970, India's Operation Flood has had an impact comparable to the green revolution on rural incomes and food prices. It has turned India's dairy sector around.

Milk consumption per person had been falling, from 39 kg in 1961 to only 32 kg in 1970. Since then it has risen rapidly, reaching 65 kg per person by 1999. Prices of milk to consumers have fallen, while the incomes of Indian dairy farmers have quadrupled.

Operation Flood was created and led by national institutions and supported by the World Bank and the EU. It began with the selling of food aid, the profits from which were used to strengthen dairy cooperatives and smallholder management. Local cows were crossed with specialized dairy breeds to produce a robust yet productive animal adapted to local conditions. Artificial insemination, veterinary services and other inputs were provided, leading to improved milk yields, longer lactation periods and shorter calving intervals. Operation Flood also focused on improving smallholders' access to markets,

opening new marketing channels for remote rural producers and thereby reducing both the need for middlemen and the seasonal variations in milk prices that had previously discouraged producers. Milk collection and chilling centres were established, minimizing waste due to spoilage.

Operation Flood has greatly helped India's rural poor. Three-fifths of the operation's 9 million producers are marginal or small-scale farmers or landless people. The impact on women has been particularly marked. Six thousand village-level Women's Dairy Cooperative Societies have been formed. As women have shifted into dairy production, they have freed up employment opportunities, especially on construction sites where they traditionally worked as unskilled labourers. Money earned from the dairy industry has been used to keep children in school. Older female siblings, relieved of the need to stay at home to care for younger children, now have the option of continuing their education.

Milk consumption in India, 1961 to 1999

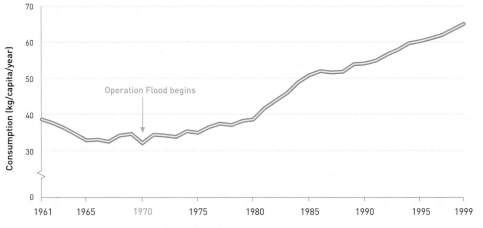

Source: FAO data

Towards sustainable forestry

Globally, deforestation is slowing down. At the same time, the productivity of timber processing is improving, helping to meet the rising demand for wood. However, hotspots of deforestation are likely to persist, undermining biodiversity and the provision of other economic and environmental benefits from forests. The major challenge will be to improve the sustainable management of forests and to ensure equitable distribution of the benefits of forest use.

Forests and other wooded areas perform key economic and ecological functions. Not only do they provide goods and livelihoods but they also protect soils, regulate water flow and retain carbon that might otherwise add to greenhouse gases. Forests also shelter much of the world's terrestrial biodiversity.

In 2000 the world had some 3 870 million ha of forests, covering 30 percent of its land area. Tropical and subtropical forests comprised 56 percent of the forest area, while temperate and boreal forests accounted for the rest. Natural forests were estimated to constitute about 95 percent of global forests, while plantation forests constitute around 5 percent.

Altogether, 51 percent of global forests are available for wood supply. Some 12 percent of forests are in legally protected areas, while the remaining 37 percent are physically inaccessible or otherwise uneconomic for wood supply.

More than half the wood biomass consumed globally is burned as fuel. Most fuel consumption occurs in developing countries, where wood is often the primary source of energy. Asia and Africa together consume more than three-quarters of global fuelwood, mostly in domestic cooking, though cottage industries such as food drying and brick-making also consume large volumes in some countries.

Industrial roundwood currently comprises about 45 percent of global wood production. Interestingly, annual per capita wood consumption in developed and developing countries is about equal, at just over 0.5 m^3 per person. However, almost 80 percent of wood consumption in developed countries is in the form of industrial wood products, while in developing countries well over 80 percent is burned as fuel.

World trade in wood does not lend itself to easy generalizations. Production and trading patterns are highly diverse, both regionally and among different commodities. In 2000, temperate and boreal zones accounted for 80 percent of world industrial roundwood production and 83 percent of roundwood exports. However, these zones also accounted for 85 percent of wood product consumption. Also in 2000, tropical areas were net exporters of wood products to the tune of around 59 million m^3 per year, though this was less than 4 percent of global consumption.

From deforestation to reforestation

It is often suggested that the world faces a deforestation crisis. Certainly, in some countries the picture is alarming and a rapid decline in forest area continues. During the 1990s, the total forest area shrank by a net 9.4 million ha each year, an area about three times the size of Belgium. Over the decade as a whole, the area lost was bigger than Nigeria.

It is true that if current deforestation rates are projected into the future, then by 2030 natural tropical forests will shrink by a further 24 percent. However, deforestation was slower in the 1990s than in the 1980s and will probably continue to slow during the first decades of the new century.

The picture varies considerably from region to region. Deforestation was most rapid in the tropics, where 1990s losses averaged 12.3 million ha per year. Africa lost 5.3 million ha a year and South America 3.7 million ha. In contrast, annual losses in Asia were only 0.4 million ha, while non-tropical areas actually added 2.9 million ha a year to their forests.

Net deforestation is now slowing in many developing countries. For more than a decade, countries such as China, India, Libyan Arab Jamahiriya, Turkey and Uruguay have planted more forest than they have cut. By 2000, other countries, such as Algeria, Bangladesh, Gambia and Viet Nam, had also begun accumulating net forest area. Some countries, for example Thailand and the Philippines, have imposed complete bans on natural forest harvesting, although these may not last and are difficult to implement. In many developing countries, population growth and dependence on agri-culture will lead to continuing loss of forests. However, overall rates of deforestation will slow further in the coming decades. Social, economic and political trends will contribute to the

> During the 1990s, the area of tropical forests shrank by a net 12.3 million ha each year, but non-tropical areas actually added 2.9 million ha a year to their forests.

slowdown in deforestation in developing countries. Urbanization will reduce the need to open up new frontier land to create livelihoods. It will also drive a shift from wood to fossil fuels and electricity.

This slowing is an integral part of the cycle of economic development. In the initial stages of development, rapidly growing populations are still heavily reliant on agriculture and fuelwood and some countries may depend on timber exports to generate foreign currency, with the result that deforestation may be rampant. As countries grow richer and more urbanized, the need to clear forests declines and the value

Forest area as a percentage of country land area

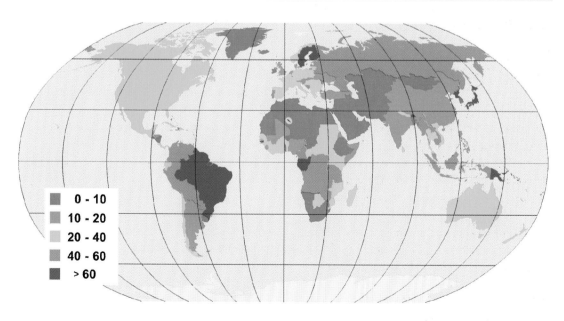

0 - 10
10 - 20
20 - 40
40 - 60
> 60

Source: FAO (2001)

placed on natural environments rises. More and more forests are protected or managed sustainably.

In developed countries, populations are growing only slowly and forest areas are mostly increasing as marginal farmland is set aside and regenerates as secondary natural forest.

Wood products: growing demand, growing productivity

Demand for forest products will continue to grow as world population and incomes grow. The most recent FAO projections estimate that by 2030 global consumption of industrial roundwood will rise by 60 percent over current levels, to around 2 400 million m³. Substantial rises are also likely in the consumption of paper and paperboard products.

Will the world's forest resources be able to cope? Until the early 1990s, expert assessments were pessimistic, but most experts today no longer foresee a crisis in the supply of wood. Projections of wood consumption are lower now, partly because of lower world population growth. In addition, there have been improvements in forest management and in harvesting and processing technologies, increases in plantation

establishment, and an expansion of the role of trees outside forests.

The production of wood-based materials is continually increasing in efficiency, reducing the pressure on forest resources. Not only is there more recycling of paper and wood. The past decade has also seen a shift from industrial roundwood and sawnwood to wood-based panels, which make much fuller use of timber. Global production of sawn timber has remained largely static since 1970, yet that of wood-based panels has more than doubled, while the production of paper and paperboard has almost tripled.

In the future, the key questions will not be whether there will be enough wood but rather where it should come from, who will produce it, and how it should be produced.

There has been a shift in the sources of wood, away from poorly regulated wild forests towards plantations and sustainably managed forests and woodlands. Industrial roundwood production from plantations is expected to double by 2030, from 400 million m³ today to around 800 million m³. Thus increased plantation supplies will meet much of the growth in demand for wood during this period.

Forest area changes (million ha), 1990 to 2000

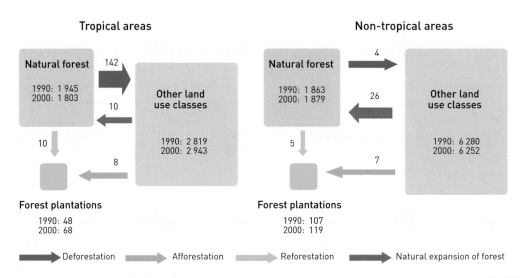

Source: FAO (2001)

Another greatly expanded source of wood will be tree cultivation outside forests.

Changes in the conditions of trade are unlikely to be dramatic, as most significant tariff barriers have already been reduced to moderate levels or completely removed — though eco-labelling and environmental regulations will doubtless increase. However, there will be major shifts in the directions of international trade, as developing countries increase their per capita consumption of industrial wood. In some of the richer countries, per capita con-sumption is currently at least tenfold that of many developing countries.

Stressing forestry's environmental services

Increasing realization of the importance of environmental values and services is helping efforts to conserve forest and tree resources. As the wider environmental services of trees are recognized, the planting or conservation of trees and forests is being fostered by develop-ment projects and programmes as a means of preventing erosion, regulating water flow and so avoiding downstream flooding, and controlling desertification or salinization. The trend towards tree and forest planting and conservation is likely to continue.

A shift in attitudes has led to a rise in the value attached to environment and nature conservation by non-governmental and development organizations. There is increasing pressure to adhere to acceptable standards of natural resource management in all efforts to stimulate economic growth and promote livelihoods for poor rural people. The emergence of democratic institutions and improved access to information are helping this process.

Shifts in consumer values, especially in the richer developed countries, have led to an increase in environmentally conscious purchasing. The spread of eco-labelling now allows consumers to choose products from sustainably managed forests.

Ecotourism is another outcome of the same shift. This is currently estimated to constitute around 7 percent of global tourism, a share that is expected to increase. Paradoxically, a high volume of ecotourists can place great pressure on sites that offer memorable experiences. Nevertheless, ecotourism can prove a valuable source of income for local communities and hence an economic incentive to conserve remaining forests.

> Measures such as reduced deforestation, forest regeneration and plantation development could reduce carbon dioxide emissions by the equivalent of 12 to 15 percent of all the emissions from fossil fuels between 1995 and 2050.

Growing concern over global warming has focused attention on the potential role of forests in regulating carbon dioxide levels in the atmosphere. Forests store large amounts of carbon in trees, understory vegetation, litter and soil. Globally, they contain some 1 200 billion tonnes of carbon, just over half the total in all terrestrial vegetation and soils.

New forests, or degraded forests that are allowed to regenerate, absorb and store carbon as they grow. Conversely, when they are cleared or degraded, forests can become a substantial source of carbon dioxide emissions. According to the Intergovernmental Panel on Climate Change (IPCC), measures such as reduced deforestation, forest regeneration and plantation development could reduce carbon dioxide emissions by the equivalent of 12 to 15 percent of all emissions from fossil fuels between 1995 and 2050. However, it is not yet clear to what extent this potential will be reflected in formal international agreements on climate change.

Sustainable forest management

The set of principles and practices known as sustainable forest management (SFM) is increasingly accepted as the core paradigm for forestry development. SFM implies broadening the focus of management from wood production to include more emphasis on equitable and participatory development and on environmental considerations.

If forest development is inequitable, the poor who are excluded from it will continue to depend on land and forest resources, but will exert greater pressure on the remaining areas to which they have access and may encroach illegally on protected areas or those allocated to large-scale enterprises. Hence an important aspect of SFM is its emphasis on providing sustainable livelihoods for the estimated 350 million of the world's poorest and most marginalized people who depend on forest ecosystems.

Non-wood forest products (NWFPs), such as wild foods, plants and medicinal herbs, are crucial to this vulnerable group. The majority are subsistence goods or are traded only in local markets. However, an estimated 150 NWFPs are traded internationally. While dependence on many subsistence products may decline, increasing demand for ethnic foods and medicines may lead to the more systematic cultivation of some NWFPs. Access to knowledge and technology will be critical if local communities are to benefit from this trend.

Under the participatory development associated with SFM, the primary responsibility of forestry departments will shift from management to policy development and regulatory functions. Responsibility for management will pass largely to the private sector, including farmers and local communities.

The environmental goals of SFM will include increasing the area of protected forest and reversing the loss of biomass, soil fertility and biodiversity that occurs when forests are degraded. Unsustainable forestry practices will be discouraged and logging techniques that reduce negative impacts on the forest as a whole will be encouraged. Improved security of land and tree tenure will encourage tree planting, both inside and outside forests.

There has been progress towards the wider adoption of SFM, though that progress has been uneven. At one end of the spectrum, forest management is carefully monitored against agreed social and environmental criteria. At the other, substantial tracts of (mainly tropical) forests are still managed poorly or not at all, leaving them vulnerable to careless or unscrupulous degradation.

Advances in remote sensing and in data processing and exchange will make it easier for national and international bodies to monitor forest management practices. But if SFM is to succeed, it will be crucial to strengthen the developing world's forestry institutions, which are still severely under-resourced.

Some non-wood forest products

End use	Typical products
Food products and additives	Wild meat, edible nuts, fruits, honey, bamboo shoots, birds' nests, oil seeds, mushrooms, palm sugar and starch, spices, culinary herbs, food colorants, gums, caterpillars and insects, fungi
Ornamental plants	Wild orchids, bulbs, cycads, palms, tree ferns, succulent plants, carnivorous plants
Animals and animal products	Plumes, pelts, cage birds, butterflies, lac, cochineal dye, cocoons, beeswax, snake venom
Construction materials	Bamboo, rattan, grass, palm, leaves, bark fibres
Organic chemicals	Phytopharmaceuticals, aromatic chemicals and flavours, fragrances, agrochemicals/insecticides, biodiesel, tans, colours, dyes

Souce: FAO data

The role of forests in protecting biodiversity

Increasingly, biodiversity is seen not just as a source of genetic material, medicines or other commercial products but as having value in itself. It has been estimated that forests, especially tropical rainforests, harbour as much as half the world's biodiversity.

Globally, more than 30 000 protected areas have been established. The goal of the World Conservation Union (IUCN) is that 10 percent of each country's land area should be under some form of protection. At present, some 80 countries have attained this level, but around 100 countries still have less than 5 percent.

The World Conservation Monitoring Centre estimates that only 6.4 percent of the area of forest biomes is under some form of protection at present — and as little as 3.6 percent in the case of temperate broad-leaf forests. These shortfalls reflect the uneven distribution of forest ecosystems among countries, in addition to an overall failure to meet the IUCN goal.

Almost 9 percent of tropical rainforests are protected, but in many developing countries this protection is only nominal. These forests continue to suffer serious encroachments, including logging, deliberate burning, poaching and other forms of clearing or degradation.

The prospects for future expansion of protected areas are more modest than in the recent past. In many countries where conservation efforts fall below the IUCN goal, there are already intense pressures on these areas and strong conflicts between economic and environmental objectives. During the next 30 years the total land area under strict protection will increase only moderately. Other means must be found to conserve biodiversity, including the on-farm production and conservation of trees and the conservation of germplasm in genebanks. Larger areas could also be placed under SFM, which affords conservation high priority as a management objective.

World fisheries: a choice of futures

The marine fisheries catch levelled off during the 1990s. Aquaculture grew rapidly, allowing continued growth in total fish production. With many marine stocks now fully exploited or overexploited, future fish supplies are likely to be constrained by resource limits. Achieving effective governance of world fisheries is crucial.

Fisheries play an important role in the world food economy. Worldwide, more than 30 million fishers and fish farmers and their families gain their livelihoods from fisheries. Most of them are poor artisanal fisher families in developing countries.

Globally, fish provide about 16 percent of the animal protein consumed by humans, and are a valuable source of minerals and essential fatty acids. Ocean and freshwater fish are also an increasingly important recreational resource, both for active users such as anglers and for passive users such as tourists, sports divers and nature-lovers.

Over the past three decades world production
of fish has more than kept pace with human
population growth, with the result that the
amount of fish available per person has
increased. The recent stagnation of capture
fisheries has been balanced by the rapid buildup of aquaculture.

Total annual fish production almost doubled
between 1970 and 1999, from 65 million tonnes
to 125 million tonnes. This rise was the outcome
of two contrasting trends: growth in capture
fisheries followed by a levelling off in the 1990s,
and dramatic growth in aquaculture during the
1990s.

Since the1950s, increases in marine capture
levels have been made possible by advances in
fishing technology and efficiency, including
synthetic fibres for fishing gear, on-board
freezing, electronic fish finding and improved
navigation. However, as more and more fishery
areas and fish stocks reached full utilization or
were overfished, the growth of marine catches
began to flatten out. During the 1990s, marine
catches fluctuated between 80 and 85 million
tonnes per year, despite the discovery of new
stocks.

> The continuing rise in overall fish
> production was made possible by the
> growth of aquaculture at 10 percent
> per year during the 1990s. The
> contribution of aquaculture to world
> fish production doubled over the
> decade, reaching 26 percent in 1999.

Catches in inland waters, however,
continued to grow moderately, from 6.4 million
tonnes per year in 1990 to 8.2 million tonnes in
1999 — though the true inland total may be
much higher, as produce is often bartered, sold
or consumed locally without being formally
recorded.

What made possible the continuing rise in
overall fish production was the rapid growth of
aquaculture, which expanded by 10 percent per
year during the 1990s. The share of aquaculture in world fish production doubled over
the decade, reaching 26 percent in 1999.

So far, aquaculture has been heavily concentrated in Asia, which provided 89 percent of
world production in 1999. A growing diversity of
species is now cultured. Until the mid-twentieth
century the range was limited to oysters,
mussels, carps, trouts and shrimps. However,
since the 1950s scientists have gradually solved
the problem of artificial reproduction for
different carps, salmonids and other species.

The overall increase in fish production has
been paralleled by a steady growth in consumption. Fish now account for an average of
30 percent of the animal protein consumed in
Asia, approximately 20 percent in Africa and
around 10 percent in Latin America and the
Caribbean. By 1999 global average intake of
fish, crustaceans and molluscs reached 16.3 kg
per person, an increase of more than 70 percent
over the 1961-63 level.

Fisheries are also a significant source of
livelihoods. In developed countries, employment
in fishing has declined due to improvements in
productivity and the collapse of some important
fisheries. In contrast, in developing countries
fisheries employment has continued to expand.
Over 90 percent of the people fully employed in
the fisheries sector in the early 1990s were in
the developing or transition economies.

Nearly 40 percent of all fish production
is now internationally traded. As a result,
fisheries are increasingly seen as a powerful
means of generating hard currency. Developing
countries' gross earnings from fish exports have
grown rapidly, from US$5.2 billion in 1985 to
US$15.6 billion in 1999, a level that far exceeds
earnings from commodities such as coffee,
cocoa, banana or rubber.

Fish consumption per person is expected to
continue to rise. If it were to be determined
solely by income growth and dietary changes,

average intake could reach as high as 22.5 kg per person by 2030. Combined with population growth, this would imply a total annual demand for fish of 186 million tonnes by 2030 — almost double the present level. However, since supply will probably be limited by environmental factors, a more likely range for demand is 150 to 160 million tonnes, or between 19 and 20 kg per person.

The regional picture will be very diverse. Health and diet quality concerns will boost consumption in North America, Europe and Oceania, but slow population growth will mean slow increase in overall demand.

In sub-Saharan Africa and the Near East and North Africa, fish consumption per person may stagnate or even decline, despite current low levels. In Africa, local wild stocks are almost fully exploited and, except in Egypt, aquaculture has barely begun. Per capita demand in South Asia, Latin America and China may increase only gradually, while in the rest of East Asia it will almost double, reaching 40 kg by 2030.

Asian aquaculturists should be able to increase production, and any remaining shortfall can be met by imports.

There is a growing trend to market fish fresh for human consumption. This is because the costs of delivering fresh fish to markets are falling and consumers are willing to pay a premium for this product. Demand for fish meal and fish oil will continue to grow rapidly. These products are used for livestock and aquaculture feeds, and at present account for about a quarter of world fish production. So far the raw material for fish meal and oil has been supplied by capture fisheries, and in all likelihood this will continue. However, the competition for small surface fish will become more intense, and the fish meal and oil industry will need to exploit other raw materials, such as mesopleagic fish and krill. Rising prices will also drive a switch to substitute feeds. However, a satisfactory replacement for fish oil has not yet been found.

Aquaculture and marine ranching will continue to expand

Over the next three decades, the world's fisheries will meet demand by continuing the same shift from fish capture to fish cultivation that gained momentum in the 1990s.

The share of capture fisheries in world production will continue to decline. The maximum sustainable marine production has been estimated at around 100 million tonnes a year. However, this is higher than the annual catches of 80 to 85 million tonnes achieved during the 1990s, and assumes that large quantities of hitherto underexploited aquatic resources will be used, including krill, mesopelagic fish and oceanic squids.

As in the 1990s, most of the shortfall will be made up by aquaculture, which will probably continue to grow at rates of 5 to 7 percent a year, at least until 2015.

Aquaculture species will be improved. Traditional breeding, chromosome manipulation and hybridization have already made significant contributions. In future the use of new technologies, such as genetic modification, can be expected. Already, a gene that codes for an anti-

Fish consumption by region, 1961-63 and 1997-99

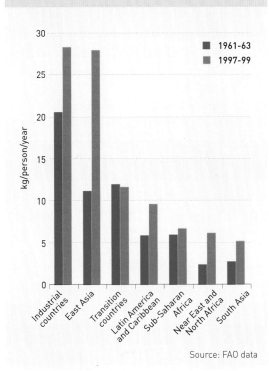

Source: FAO data

freeze protein in the Arctic flounder has been transferred to Atlantic salmon to increase its tolerance of cold waters. Currently, however, no commercial aquaculture producer is marketing such transgenic species for human consumption. If this field is to progress, public concerns about GM organisms will need to be addressed through risk assessments and the development of policy guidelines for responsible use.

Additional species will be domesticated for aquaculture. For halibut, cod and tuna, which have been fished in high volumes in capture fisheries, aquaculture production could eventually be high. If commercially viable technology is developed soon, by 2015 the cultured production of cod could reach 1 to 2 million tonnes per year.

Environmental concerns will probably shift the focus of aquaculture away from coastal zones into more intensive inland systems. Marine ranching will also expand, though its long-term future will depend on solutions to the problems of ownership surrounding released animals. At present, only Japan is engaged in sea ranching on a large scale.

Social and political pressure will also drive efforts to reduce the impact of capture fisheries, for example by making use of the unwanted catch of non-target species and by using more selective fishing gear and practices. Increasing use of eco-labels will enable consumers to choose sustainably harvested fish products, a trend which will encourage environmentally sensitive approaches in the industry.

Towards sustainable fisheries

The single most important influence on the future of wild capture fisheries is their governance. Although in theory renewable, wild fishery resources are in practice finite for production purposes. If they are overexploited, production declines and may even collapse.

Resources must therefore be harvested at sustainable levels. In addition, access must be equitably shared among producers. As fish resources grow increasingly scarce, conflicts over access are becoming more frequent.

The principal policy challenge is to bring the capacity of the global fishing fleet back to a level at which fish stocks can be harvested sustainably. Past policies have promoted the buildup of excess capacity and incited fishermen to increase the catch beyond sustainable levels. Policy makers must act fast to reverse this situation.

There are numerous measures that could encourage sustainable use and remove the perverse incentives to overfish. Fisheries based on clearly defined rights of access will need to become more common: experience shows that when these rights are not merely in place but are understood and observed by users, conflicts tend to be minimized.

Laws and institutions need to be established or strengthened to limit and control access to marine fish stocks, both by larger ocean-going

The maximum sustainable marine production is estimated at around 100 million tonnes a year, compared to annual catches of 80 to 85 million tonnes in the 1990s. But the estimate assumes that large quantities of hitherto underexploited resources will be used, including krill and oceanic squids.

State of the world's fishery stocks, 1998

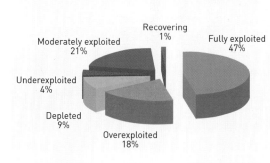

Source: FAO data

The changing ecology of the oceans

Biodiversity comprises four main elements: variability within species, among species, among ecosystems and among larger ecological complexes. It is a key ingredient of sustainable fisheries in the future.

Altogether, over 1 100 species of fish, mollusc and crustacean are taken in capture fisheries, while over 300 species are used in aquaculture. Biodiversity in wild populations allows adaptation to the changing environment, while in farmed fish it allows continued breed improvement.

Human fishing activities have had a powerful impact on aquatic biodiversity. The current high level of impact may limit capture fishing in future, unless the governance and management of ocean and freshwater resources are greatly improved.

Damage is done by several unsustainable fishing practices. These include: the use of poison and dynamite near coral reefs; nonselective fishing gears that capture marine mammals, unwanted species or fish that are too small; and bottom trawling, which disturbs the ecology of the ocean floor.

Perhaps the major ecological impact stems from the sheer extent of human fishing. Many fishing areas and stocks are fished up to or beyond the sustainable limit, while fishing pressure appears to have altered the distribution and size of some fish.

The overall impact on ocean ecology is only sketchily known, but appears to be significant. Statistics on fish landings suggest that there has been a reduction in the numbers of larger predatory fish, shifting the balance of catches towards fish that eat lower down the food chain. As high-value species such as bottom-dwellers or large surface fish such as tuna are overfished, they are gradually replaced by shorter-lived and smaller surface-dwelling and schooling fish. Numbers of smaller fish are also boosted in some areas by increased plankton production.

By 1998, some 12 out of the FAO's 16 world fishing regions had production levels at or below their historical maximum. Indeed, the Antarctic, the Southeast and Northwest Atlantic and the Southeast Pacific had fallen below half their maximum past production levels.

In terms of stocks of main species, FAO estimates suggest that, by the end of the 1990s, only a quarter of stocks were moderately exploited or underexploited and 1 percent were recovering. Nearly half of all stocks were exploited up to their maximum sustainable yield and were thus potentially on the brink of being overexploited. More than a quarter of stocks were overfished or depleted.

Such developments have raised concern among environmentalists and other stakeholder groups. In response, fishery administrations are working to minimize or mitigate the negative impacts on genetic and biological diversity. Measures include the development and use of selective fishing gears that reduce the capture of marine mammals, undersized target species and unwanted bycatch, direct controls on the total catch allowed of various species and, in some cases, outright fishing bans and moratoriums.

Unfortunately, inappropriate fishing and aquaculture activities are only one of the threats to aquatic biodiversity. Additional threats include pollution, loss of habitat and habitat degradation. Such threats often combine to aggravate pressure on biodiversity. The whole range of threats must be addressed if aquatic biodiversity is to be protected.

vessels and by local artisanal fishers. Increasingly, the responsibility for managing fisheries will have to be devolved to fishing interests and other stakeholder groups. Traditional arrangements in fishing communities can be incorporated into new management regimes. However, the need to control entry into artisanal fisheries will become more pressing. Indeed, if this issue is not tackled, a large number of fisher households may be forced out of fishery and, unless there are alternative livelihoods, into poverty.

If the world's fisheries are to achieve their full potential, the major policy and management challenges must be met, and the cultural and social concerns of all stakeholder groups must be addressed. These are enormous challenges, yet they are not insurmountable.

Prospects for the Environment

Agriculture and the environment

Previous sections of this report have already discussed the environmental aspects of agriculture as they relate to each sector. This section discusses the overarching or cross-sectoral environmental issues and provides an overview of the major trends in agriculture that can be expected to affect the environment over the next 30 years.

Over the next 30 years, many agriculture-related environmental problems will remain serious. However, some problems may deepen more slowly than in the past and some may even be reversed.

Agriculture has a vast impact on the earth
Agriculture accounts for the major share of human use of land. Pasture and crops alone took up 37 percent of the earth's land area in 1999. Over two-thirds of human water use is for agriculture. In Asia the share is four-fifths.

Crop and livestock production have a profound effect on the wider environment. They are the main source of water pollution by nitrates, phosphates and pesticides. They are also the major anthropogenic source of the greenhouse gases methane and nitrous oxide, and contribute on a massive scale to other types of air and water pollution. The extent and methods of agriculture, forestry and fishing are the leading causes of loss of the world's biodiversity. The overall external costs of all three sectors can be considerable.

Agriculture also affects the basis for its own future through land degradation, salinization, the overextraction of water and the reduction of genetic diversity in crops and livestock. However, the long-term consequences of these processes are difficult to quantify.

If more sustainable production methods are used, the negative impacts of agriculture on the environment can be attenuated. Indeed, in some cases agriculture can play an important role in reversing them, for example by storing carbon in soils, enhancing the infiltration of water and preserving rural landscapes and biodiversity.

Percentage of annual nitrogen emissions from different sources

Ocean 20%
Natural soils 40%
Industrial sources 9%
Biomass burning 3%
Cattle 14%
Agricultural soils 14%

Total emissions: 15 million tonnes per year

Source: Adapted from Mosier and Kroeze (1998)

Fertilizers, manure and pesticides are major causes of water pollution

Pollution of groundwater by agricultural chemicals and wastes is a major issue in almost all developed countries and, increasingly, in many developing countries.

Pollution from fertilizers occurs when these are applied more heavily than crops can absorb or when they are washed or blown off the soil surface before they can be incorporated. Excess nitrogen and phosphates can leach into groundwater or run off into waterways. This nutrient overload causes eutrophication of lakes, reservoirs and ponds, leading to an explosion of algae which suppress other aquatic plants and animals.

The crop projections to 2030 imply a slower growth of nitrogen fertilizer use than in the past. If efficiency can be improved, the increase in total fertilizer use between 1997-99 and 2030 could be as low as 37 percent. However, current use in many developing countries is very inefficient. In China, the world's largest consumer of nitrogen fertilizer, up to half the nitrogen applied is lost by volatilization and another 5 to 10 percent by leaching.

Insecticides, herbicides and fungicides are also applied heavily in many developed and developing countries, polluting fresh water with carcinogens and other poisons that affect humans and many forms of wildlife. Pesticides also reduce biodiversity by destroying weeds and insects and hence the food species of birds and other animals.

Pesticide use has increased considerably over the past 35 years, with recent growth rates of 4 to 5.4 percent in some regions. The 1990s showed signs of declining use of insecticides, both in developed countries such as France, Germany and the United Kingdom and in a few developing countries, such as India. In contrast, herbicide use continued to rise in most countries.

As concern about pollution and the loss of biodiversity grows, future use of pesticides may grow more slowly than in the past. In developed countries, use is increasingly restrained by regulations and taxes. In addition, use will be curbed by the growing demand for organic crops, produced without chemical inputs. The future is likely to see increasing use of "smart" pesticides, resistant crop varieties and ecological methods of pest control (IPM).

Agriculture as a cause of air pollution

Agriculture is also a source of air pollution. It is the dominant anthropogenic source of ammonia. Livestock account for about 40 percent of global emissions, mineral fertilizers for 16 percent and biomass burning and crop residues for about 18 percent.

Ammonia is even more acidifying than sulphur dioxide and nitrogen oxides. It is one of the major causes of acid rain, which damages trees, acidifies soils, lakes and rivers, and harms biodiversity. As other acidifying gases such as sulphur dioxide are brought under tighter control, ammonia may in time become the leading cause of acidification. Emissions of ammonia from agriculture are likely to continue rising in both developed and developing countries. The livestock projections imply a 60 percent increase in ammonia emissions from animal excreta.

The burning of plant biomass is another major source of air pollutants, including carbon dioxide, nitrous oxide and smoke particles. It is estimated that humans are responsible for about 90 percent of biomass burning, mainly through the deliberate burning of forest vegetation in association with deforestation and of pastures and crop residues to promote regrowth and destroy pest habitats. The massive forest fires in Southeast Asia in 1997 burned at least 4.5 million ha and covered the region with a pall of smoke and haze. The burning of tropical savannas is estimated to destroy three

Projections suggest that, by 2030, emissions of ammonia and methane from the livestock sector of developing countries could be at least 60 percent higher than at present.

times as much dry biomass each year as the burning of tropical forests.

Pressures on biodiversity

As their numbers and needs have grown, human beings have taken up an increasing share of the planet's surface area and resources for their own needs, often displacing other species in the process. Estimates of the total number of species on earth vary wildly. The number that has been scientifically described is around 1.75 million, but the true total is unknown and may be anything from 7 to 20 million or more. Estimates of losses of biodiversity to extinction over the coming decades vary widely, from 2 to 25 percent of all species.

> Loss of biodiversity owing to agricultural methods continues unabated, even in countries where nature is highly valued and protected.

Agriculture, forestry and fisheries are perhaps the most significant of human pressures on the biodiversity of land and sea.

Species richness is closely related to the area of a wild habitat. As the area declines, so does the number of species it harbours, though at a slower rate. Deforestation, field consolidation, with the accompanying reduction in field margins and hedgerows, and drainage of wetlands for farming reduce the overall area available for wildlife and fragment natural habitats. Grazing lowers species richness in pastures.

Agricultural intensification adds its own problems. Pesticides and herbicides directly destroy many insects and unwanted plants, and reduce food supplies for higher animals. Hence loss of biodiversity is not limited to the land clearing stage of agricultural development but continues long afterwards. It is unabated even in developed countries where nature is highly valued and protected.

Some of the affected life forms may be important soil nutrient recyclers, crop pollinators and predators of pests. Others are potentially a major source of genetic material for improving domesticated crops and livestock.

The pressures on biodiversity over the next three decades will be the outcome of conflicting trends. Extensive methods will tend to give way to intensification, which may in turn give way to organic agriculture or to NT/CA.

Loss of wildlife habitat to farming will continue, but at a slower pace. Deforestation will slow down, and extensive grazing will give way increasingly to industrial livestock production. Although intensification entails its own range of environmental risks related to pesticides, chemical fertilizers and animal wastes, the increasing inclusion of environmental considerations in agricultural policy will help to counteract these.

Reducing agriculture's pollution toll

The spread of NT/CA will help to improve soil structure and reduce erosion. IPM will reduce pesticide use, while programmes to improve the management of plant nutrition should reduce the overuse of chemical fertilizers.

Other policies will help to reduce the conflict between agricultural intensification and environmental protection. Tighter regulations and national strategies on the management of animal waste and the use of chemical fertilizers and pesticides may be required, along with the removal of subsidies on chemical and fossil energy inputs. Pesticides should be subjected to more rigorous testing, and residue buildup more closely monitored.

> Agriculture is an increasingly significant source of greenhouse gases, as well as a potential route to the mitigation of climate change through carbon storage in soils and vegetation.

Agriculture and climate change

Agriculture as source and sink

Agriculture is a major source of greenhouse gas emissions. It releases large quantities of carbon dioxide through the burning of biomass, mainly in areas of deforestation and grassland.

Agriculture is also responsible for up to half of all methane emissions. Though it persists for a shorter time in the atmosphere, methane is about 20 times more powerful than carbon dioxide in its warming action and is therefore a major short-term contributor to global warming. Current annual anthropogenic emissions are around 540 million tonnes and are growing at around 5 percent per year.

Livestock alone account for about a quarter of methane emissions, by way of gut fermentation and the decay of excreta. As livestock numbers grow, and as livestock rearing becomes increasingly industrial, the production of manure is projected to rise by about 60 percent by 2030. Methane emissions from livestock are likely to increase by the same proportion.

Irrigated rice farming is the other main agricultural source of methane, accounting for about a fifth of total anthropogenic emissions. The area used for irrigated rice is projected to increase by about 10 percent by 2030. However, emissions may grow more slowly, because an increasing share of rice will be grown with better controlled irrigation and nutrient management, and rice varieties may be used which emit less methane.

Agriculture is a key source of another important greenhouse gas: nitrous oxide. This is generated by natural processes, but is boosted by leaching, volatilization and runoff of nitrogen fertilizers, and by the breakdown of crop residues and animal wastes. Livestock account for about half of anthropogenic emissions. Annual nitrous oxide emissions from agriculture are projected to grow by 50 percent by 2030.

Agriculture can help mitigate climate change

Farming can also be a sink for carbon. However, it is generally believed that soils, like other biological sinks (e.g. vegetation), have an inherent upper limit for storage. The total amount that can be stored is crop- and location-specific and the rate of sequestration declines after a few years of growth before eventually reaching this limit. In 1997-99 an estimated 590 to 1 180 million tonnes of carbon were locked up in cropland soils alone, in the form of soil organic matter from crop residues and manure. Projections of increased crop production imply that by 2030 this total could rise by 50 percent.

Other changes could boost the total even further. If only 2 million of the current 126 million ha of saline soils were restored each year, they could account for an extra 13 million tonnes of carbon annually. In developed countries, permanent set-aside land can sequester large amounts of carbon if it is left unmanaged, or reforested.

Depending on agroclimatic conditions, NT/CA can lock up 0.1 to 1 tonne of carbon per ha per year, in addition to cutting carbon dioxide emissions by over 50 percent through the reduced use of fossil fuel in ploughing. The growth potential for NT/CA is considerable. If another 150 million ha of rainfed cropland is converted to NT/CA by 2030 and the average sequestration rate on land managed in this way is 0.2 to 0.4 tonne per ha per year, a further 30 to 60 million tonnes of carbon could be soaked up annually during the first few years after conversion.

Should any of these practices be discontinued, the sequestered carbon would be released over a period of a few years. Agricultural carbon sinks of this kind are needed to "buy time" in which to cope with carbon dioxide emissions at source.

Climate change will have very diverse impacts on agriculture

Climate change will affect agriculture, forestry and fisheries in complex ways, positive as well as negative.

Global carbon dioxide concentrations in the atmosphere are expected to rise from 350 ppm

In the next three decades, climate change is not expected to depress global food availability, but it may increase the dependence of developing countries on food imports and accentuate food insecurity for vulnerable groups and countries.

to over 400 ppm by 2030. Carbon dioxide causes plant stomata to narrow, so water losses are reduced and the efficiency of water use improves. Increasing atmospheric concentrations of carbon dioxide will also stimulate photosynthesis and have a fertilizing effect on many crops.

Average global temperatures are projected to rise by between 1.4 and 5.8 °C by 2100. By 2030 the increase will be rather lower than this, between 0.5 and 1 °C.

The rise will be greater in temperate latitudes. Here global warming may bring benefits for agriculture. The areas suitable for cropping will expand, the length of the growing period will increase, the costs of overwintering livestock will fall, crop yields will improve and forests may grow faster. These gains may, however, have to be set against the loss of some fertile land to flooding, particularly on coastal plains.

In less well-watered areas, especially in the tropics, the rise in temperatures will increase evapotranspiration and lower soil moisture levels. Some cultivated areas will become unsuitable for cropping and some tropical grasslands may become increasingly arid.

Temperature rise will also expand the range of many agricultural pests and increase the ability of pest populations to survive the winter and attack spring crops. In oceans, temperature rise may reduce plankton growth, bleach coral reefs and disrupt fish breeding and feeding patterns. Cold-water species such as cod may find their range reduced.

Higher global temperatures will also bring higher rainfall. However, this will be unevenly distributed between regions. Indeed, some tropical areas such as South Asia and northern Latin America are projected to receive less rainfall than before.

The climate is also expected to become more variable than at present, with increases in the frequency and severity of extreme events such as cyclones, floods, hailstorms and droughts. These will bring greater fluctuations in crop yields and local food supplies and higher risks of landslides and erosion damage.

Mean sea level is projected to rise by 15 to 20 cm by 2030 and by 50 cm by 2100. The rise will lead to the loss of low-lying land through flooding, seawater intrusions and storm surges. Subsidence due to the overextraction of groundwater may exacerbate the intrusion problem in some areas. There will also be damage to vegetable growing and aquaculture in low-lying areas and to fisheries dependent on mangrove swamps for their spawning grounds. The impact will be most serious in coastal zones, especially heavily populated deltas used for agriculture, of the kind found in Bangladesh, China, Egypt, India and mainland Southeast Asia. In India alone, losses by 2030 could range from 1 000 to 2 000 km^2, destroying perhaps 70 000 to 150 000 livelihoods.

There are still considerable uncertainties in most of the projections. The overall effect on global food production by 2030 is likely to be small: cereal yields, for example, are projected to decline by about 0.5 percent by the 2020s. But there will be large regional variations: in temperate regions an increase in yields is thought possible; in East Asia, the Sahel and Southern Africa the outcome could be either positive or negative; in other developing regions a decline in yields is thought more likely. In all of these cases the potential yield changes are up or down by 2.5 percent or less by 2030 and by 5 percent or less by 2050.

It is important to note that these are only the changes that may result from global warming *in the absence of any other factors*. In practice, changes in technology are likely to reduce or outweigh the impact of climate change. Among the most important technological changes will be improved crop varieties and cropping practices, which will raise yields. Factors such as the spread of NT/CA and the expansion of irrigation will combine with the dissemination of new crop varieties to reduce the sensitivity of some systems to climate change.

Inequalities in food security may accentuate
Overall, global warming seems likely to benefit agriculture in developed countries located in temperate zones but to have an adverse effect on production in many developing countries in tropical and subtropical zones. Hence climate change could increase the dependency of developing countries on imports and accentuate existing North-South differences in food security.

Some future trends will cushion the blow. Improved communications and roads will allow

Technology and policy choices

Many of the measures needed to reduce or adapt to climate change are valuable in coping with existing problems such as water and air pollution, soil erosion, and vulnerability to droughts or floods.

Measures to reduce greenhouse gas emissions:
- Removal of subsidies and introduction of environmental taxes on chemical fertilizers and energy inputs
- Improvement of fertilizer use efficiency
- Development of rice varieties emitting less methane
- Improved management of livestock waste
- Restoration of degraded lands
- Improvement of crop residue management
- Expansion of agroforestry and reforestation

Measures to promote adaptation to climate change:
- Development and distribution of crop varieties and livestock breeds resistant to drought, storms and floods, higher temperatures and saline conditions
- Improvement of water use efficiency through:
  - No-till/conservation agriculture in rainfed areas
  - Appropriate water pricing, management and technology in irrigated areas
- Promotion of agroforestry to increase ecosystem resilience and maintain biodiversity
- Maintenance of livestock mobility in pastoral areas subject to drought

Measures to reduce food insecurity:
- Reduction of rural and urban poverty
- Improvement of transport and communications in areas vulnerable to disasters
- Development of early-warning and storm-forecasting systems
- Preparedness plans for relief and rehabilitation
- Introduction of flood- and storm-resistant and salt-tolerant crops
- Introduction of land use systems to stabilize slopes and reduce the risk of soil erosion and mudslides
- Building of homes, livestock shelters and food stores above likely flood levels.

food to be transported more quickly into drought- or flood-affected areas. Economic growth and rising incomes will still allow most people in most countries to improve their nutrition levels. A continuing shift out of agricultural occupations into industry and services, and out of rural and marginal areas into urban centres, will leave fewer countries unable to pay for food imports, and fewer people vulnerable to local declines in food production.

But the food security of poor people and countries could well be reduced by climate change. Even by 2030 there will still be hundreds of millions of such people, who will be either undernourished or on the brink of undernourishment. They will be especially vulnerable to disruption of their incomes or food supply by crop failure or by extreme events such as drought and floods.

As long as agricultural trade is not entirely free and communications with marginal areas remain poor, differences between local, national and international prices will persist, with the result that food prices in areas hit by extreme events could rise steeply, even if only temporarily. For example, in the south of Mozambique maize prices in the spring of 2000 increased rapidly following the floods, while in the north they remained at half the level in the

south or even declined somewhat, because transport between the two zones was difficult.

The adverse impacts of climate change will fall disproportionately on the poor. Hardest hit will be small-scale farmers and other low-income groups in areas prone to drought, flooding, salt water intrusion or sea surges, and fishers affected by falling catches caused by higher sea temperatures and shifts in currents. The areas most likely to suffer increased climate variability and extreme events are mostly those that are already handicapped by these same phenomena. Many of the areas at risk from rising sea levels are currently poor and may not enjoy the economic development necessary to pay for flood protection.

The problem of increased vulnerability to food insecurity caused by climate change is likely to be most serious in some 30 to 40 countries. Major concern centres on Africa. Some estimate that, even as early as 2020 or 2030, climate change could depress cereal production in this region by 2 to 3 percent, enough to increase the numbers at risk of hunger by 10 million. This is the projected effect *in the absence of other changes* and could be offset by even a modest annual increase in yields, but it still represents an additional hurdle that agriculture in Africa must leap.

Annex 1

Countries and commodities covered

Developing countries

Africa, sub-Saharan	Latin America and Caribbean	Near East and North Africa	South Asia	East Asia
Angola	Argentina	Afghanistan	Bangladesh	Cambodia
Benin	Bolivia	Algeria	India	China
Botswana	Brazil	Egypt	Maldives	Dem. Rep. of Korea
Burkina Faso	Chile	Iran, Islamic Rep.	Nepal	Indonesia
Burundi	Colombia	Iraq	Pakistan	Lao People's Dem. Rep.
Cameroon	Costa Rica	Jordan	Sri Lanka	Malaysia
Central Afr. Rep.	Cuba	Lebanon		Mongolia
Chad	Dominican Rep.	Libyan Arab Yam.		Myanmar
Congo	Ecuador	Morocco		Philippines
Côte d'Ivoire	El Salvador	Saudi Arabia		Rep. of Korea
Dem. Rep. of Congo	Guatemala	Syrian Arab Rep.		Thailand
Eritrea	Guyana	Tunisia		Viet Nam
Ethiopia	Haiti	Turkey		East Asia, other [4]
Gabon	Honduras	Yemen		
Gambia	Jamaica	Near East, other [3]		
Ghana	Mexico			
Guinea	Nicaragua			
Kenya	Panama			
Lesotho	Paraguay			
Liberia	Peru			
Madagascar	Suriname			
Malawi	Trinidad and Tobago			
Mali	Uruguay			
Mauritania	Venezuela			
Mauritius	Latin America, other [2]			
Mozambique				
Namibia				
Niger				
Nigeria				
Rwanda				
Senegal				
Sierra Leone				
Somalia				
Sudan				
Swaziland				
Togo				
Uganda				
United Rep. of Tanzania				
Zambia				
Zimbabwe				
Sub-Saharan Africa,other [1]				

---

1 Cape Verde, Comoros, Djibouti, Guinea Bissau, Sao Tomé and Principe, Seychelles.
2 Antigua, Bahamas, Barbados, Belize, Bermuda, Dominica, Grenada, Netherland Antilles, Saint Kitts and Nevis, Saint Lucia, Saint Vincent/Grenadines.
3 Cyprus, Kuwait, United Arab Emirates.
4 Brunei, Macau, Solomon Islands, Fiji, French Polynesia, New Caledonia, Vanuatu, Papua New Guinea, Kiribati.

Countries and commodities covered (continued)

Industrial countries

European Union[1]	Other Western Europe	North America	Oceania	Other
Austria	Iceland	Canada	Australia	Israel
Belgium	Malta	United States	New Zealand	Japan
Denmark	Norway			South Africa
Finland	Switzerland			
France				
Germany				
Greece				
Ireland				
Italy				
Luxembourg				
Netherlands				
Portugal				
Spain				
Sweden				
United Kingdom				

1 In the analysis the European Union was treated as one country group (EU-15).

Transition countries

Eastern Europe and the former Yugoslavia SFR	Commonwealth of Independent States	Baltic States
Albania	Armenia	Estonia
Bosnia and Herzegovina	Azerbaijan	Latvia
Bulgaria	Belarus	Lithuania
Croatia	Georgia	
Czech Republic	Kazakhstan	
Hungary	Kyrgyzstan	
Poland	Moldova Republic	
Romania	Russian Federation	
Slovakia	Tajikistan	
Slovenia	Turkmenistan	
The Former Yugoslav Rep. of Macedonia	Ukraine	
Yugoslavia, Fed. Rep.	Uzbekistan	

Countries and commodities covered (continued)

Commodities

Crops	Livestock

Crops

Wheat
Rice (paddy)
Maize
Barley
Millet
Sorghum
Other cereals
Potato
Sweet potato and yams
Cassava
Other roots
Plantains
Sugar, raw[1]
Pulses
Vegetables
Bananas
Citrus fruit
Other fruit
Vegetable oil and oilseeds (in vegetable oil equivalent)[2]
Cocoa bean
Coffee
Tea
Tobacco
Cotton lint
Jute and hard fibres
Rubber

Livestock

Beef, veal and buffalo meat
Mutton, lamb and goat meat
Pig meat
Poultry meat
Milk and dairy products   (in whole milk equivalent)
Eggs

---

1 Sugar production in the developing countries was analysed separately for sugar cane and sugar beet.
2 Vegetable oil production in the developing countries was analysed separately for soybean, groundnut, sesame seed, coconut, sunflower seed, palm oil/palm-kernel oil, rapeseed and all other oilseeds.

Note

All commodity data and projections in this report are expressed in terms of primary product equivalent unless stated otherwise. Historical commodity balances (Supply Utilization Accounts - SUAs) are available for about 160 primary and 170 processed crop and livestock commodities. To reduce this amount of information to manageable proportions, all the SUA data were converted to the commodity specification given above in the list of commodities, applying appropriate conversion factors (and ignoring joint products to avoid double counting: e.g. wheat flour is converted back into wheat while wheat bran is ignored). In this way, one SUA in homogeneous units is derived for each of the commodities of the study.

Meat production refers to indigenous meat production, i.e. production from slaughtered animals plus the meat equivalent of live animal exports minus the meat equivalent of all live animal imports. Cereals demand and trade data include the grain equivalent of beer consumption and trade.

The commodities for which SUAs were constructed are the 26 crops and 6 livestock products given in the list above. The production analysis for the developing countries was, however, carried out for 34 crops because sugar and vegetable oils were analysed separately (for production analysis only) for the 10 crops shown in the footnote to the list.

Annex 2

Total population

	Millions					Annual increments (millions)			
	1979-81	1997-99	2015	2030	2050	1995 to 2000	2010 to 2015	2025 to 2030	2045 to 2050
World (UN)[1]	4 430	5 900	7 207	8 270	9 322	79	76	67	43
World (FBS)	4 416	5 878	7 176	8 229	9 270	78	76	66	43
Developing countries	3 245	4 573	5 827	6 869	7 935	74	74	66	45
Sub-Saharan Africa	345	574	883	1 229	1 704	15	20	24	23
Near East and North Africa	238	377	520	651	809	8	9	9	7
Latin America and Car.	357	498	624	717	799	8	7	6	3
South Asia	885	1 283	1 672	1 969	2 258	23	22	19	12
East Asia	1 420	1 840	2 128	2 303	2 365	20	16	9	-1
Industrial countries	789	892	951	979	986	5	2	1	0
Transition countries	382	413	398	381	349	0	-1	-1	-2

Growth rates (% per year)

	Population					Total GDP		Per capita GDP	
	1969 to 1999	1979 to 1999	1989 to 1999	1997-99 to 2015	2015 to 2030	1997-99 to 2015	2015 to 2030	1997-99 to 2015	2015 to 2030
World (FBS)	1.7	1.6	1.5	1.2	0.9	3.5	3.8	2.3	2.9
Developing countries	2.0	1.9	1.7	1.4	1.1	5.1	5.5	3.7	4.4
Sub-Saharan Africa	2.9	2.9	2.7	2.6	2.2	4.4	4.5	1.8	2.3
Near East and North Africa	2.7	2.6	2.4	1.9	1.5	3.7	3.9	1.8	2.4
Latin America and Car.	2.1	1.9	1.7	1.3	0.9	4.1	4.4	2.8	3.5
South Asia	2.2	2.1	1.9	1.6	1.1	5.5	5.4	3.9	4.3
East Asia	1.6	1.5	1.2	0.9	0.5	6.1	6.3	5.3	5.8
Industrial countries	0.7	0.7	0.7	0.4	0.2	3.0	3.0	2.6	2.8
Transition countries	0.6	0.5	0.1	-0.2	-0.3	3.7	4.0	4.0	4.3

1 World (UN) covers all countries; World (FBS) covers all countries for which FAO Food Balance Sheet data are available.

Sources: Population: UN (2001)
GDP to 2015: World Bank (2001b)

Table A2 Growth rates of aggregate demand and production (percent per annum)

	1969 to 1999	1979 to 1999	1989 to 1999	1997-99 to 2015	2015 to 2030	1997-99 to 2030
Demand						
World	2.2	2.1	2.0	1.6	1.4	1.5
Developing countries	3.7	3.7	4.0	2.2	1.7	2.0
Idem, excl. China	3.2	3.0	3.0	2.4	2.0	2.2
Sub-Saharan Africa	2.8	3.1	3.2	2.9	2.8	2.9
Idem, excl. Nigeria	2.5	2.4	2.5	3.1	2.9	3.0
Near East and North Africa	3.8	3.0	2.7	2.4	2.0	2.2
Latin America and Caribbean	2.9	2.7	3.0	2.1	1.7	1.9
Idem, excl. Brazil	2.4	2.1	2.8	2.2	1.8	2.0
South Asia	3.2	3.3	3.0	2.6	2.0	2.3
East Asia	4.5	4.7	5.2	1.8	1.3	1.6
Idem, excl. China	3.5	3.2	2.8	2.0	1.7	1.9
Industrial countries	1.1	1.0	1.0	0.7	0.6	0.7
Transition countries	-0.2	-1.7	-4.4	0.5	0.4	0.5
Production						
World	2.2	2.1	2.0	1.6	1.3	1.5
Developing countries	3.5	3.7	3.9	2.0	1.7	1.9
Idem, excl. China	3.0	3.0	2.9	2.3	2.0	2.1
Sub-Saharan Africa	2.3	3.0	3.0	2.8	2.7	2.7
Idem, excl. Nigeria	2.0	2.2	2.4	2.9	2.7	2.8
Near East and North Africa	3.1	3.0	2.9	2.1	1.9	2.0
Latin America and Caribbean	2.8	2.6	3.1	2.1	1.7	1.9
Idem, excl. Brazil	2.3	2.1	2.8	2.1	1.8	2.0
South Asia	3.1	3.4	2.9	2.5	1.9	2.2
East Asia	4.4	4.6	5.0	1.7	1.3	1.5
Idem, excl. China	3.3	2.9	2.4	1.9	1.8	1.9
Industrial countries	1.3	1.0	1.4	0.8	0.6	0.7
Transition countries	-0.4	-1.7	-4.7	0.6	0.6	0.6
Population						
World	1.7	1.6	1.5	1.2	0.9	1.1
Developing countries	2.0	1.9	1.7	1.4	1.1	1.3
Idem, excl. China	2.3	2.2	2.0	1.7	1.3	1.5
Sub-Saharan Africa	2.9	2.9	2.7	2.6	2.2	2.4
Idem, excl. Nigeria	2.9	2.9	2.7	2.6	2.3	2.4
Near East and North Africa	2.7	2.6	2.4	1.9	1.5	1.7
Latin America and Caribbean	2.1	1.9	1.7	1.3	0.9	1.1
Idem, excl. Brazil	2.1	1.9	1.8	1.4	1.0	1.2
South Asia	2.2	2.1	1.9	1.6	1.1	1.3
East Asia	1.6	1.5	1.2	0.9	0.5	0.7
Idem, excl. China	2.0	1.8	1.6	1.2	0.9	1.0
Industrial countries	0.7	0.7	0.7	0.4	0.2	0.3
Transition countries	0.6	0.5	0.1	-0.2	-0.3	-0.2

Table A3 Per capita food consumption and undernourishment

Food consumption (kcal/capita/day)

	1964-66	1974-76	1984-86	1997-99	2015	2030
World	2 358	2 435	2 655	2 803	2 940	3 050
Developing countries	2 054	2 152	2 450	2 681	2 850	2 980
Sub-Saharan Africa	2 058	2 079	2 057	2 195	2 360	2 540
Idem, excl. Nigeria	2 037	2 076	2 057	2 052	2 230	2 420
Near East and North Africa	2 290	2 591	2 953	3 006	3 090	3 170
Latin America and Caribbean	2 393	2 546	2 689	2 824	2 980	3 140
South Asia	2 017	1 986	2 205	2 403	2 700	2 900
East Asia	1 957	2 105	2 559	2 921	3 060	3 190
Industrial countries	2 947	3 065	3 206	3 380	3 440	3 500
Transition countries	3 222	3 385	3 379	2 906	3 060	3 180

Incidence of undernourishment, developing countries

	% population				Million people			
	1990-92	1997-99	2015	2030	1990-92	1997-99	2015	2030
Developing countries	20	17	11	6	815	776	610	443
Sub-Saharan Africa	35	34	23	15	168	194	205	183
Idem, excl. Nigeria	40	40	28	18	156	186	197	178
Near East and North Africa	8	9	7	5	25	32	37	34
Latin America and Caribbean	13	11	6	4	59	54	40	25
South Asia	26	24	12	6	289	303	195	119
East Asia	16	11	6	4	275	193	135	82

Population living in countries with given per capita food consumption (million)

kcal/capita/day			Population (million)			
	1964-66	1974-76	1984-86	1997-99	2015	2030
Under 2200	1 893[1]	2 281[1]	558	571	462	196
2200-2500	288	307	1 290[2]	1 487[2]	541	837
2500-2700	154	141	1 337[3]	222	351	352
2700-3000	302	256	306	1 134	2 397[2]	2 451[2]
Over 3000	688	1 069	1 318	2 464[3]	3 425[3]	4 392[3]
World total	3 325	4 053	4 810	5 878	7 176	8 229

1 Includes India and China.
2 Includes India.
3 Includes China.

Developing countries with a given percentage of undernourishment[4]

	Population (million)			kcal/capita/day			% of population			Million people		
	1997-99	2015	2030	1997-99	2015	2030	1997-99	2015	2030	1997-99	2015	2030
Under 5%	349	1 158	5 129	3 187	3 130	3 150	2	3	3	8	37	178
5-10%	1 989	2 162	524	2 999	3 066	2 758	8	6	7	167	134	38
10-25%	1 632	1 939	948	2 434	2 644	2 411	21	13	16	349	250	155
Over 25%	586	544	239	1 988	2 085	2 149	43	35	30	251	190	72
Total	4 555	5 804	6 840	2 681	2 850	2 980	17	11	6	776	611	443

4 Different countries form each group in the different years.

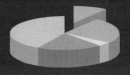

Table A4 Changes in commodity composition of food

	Cereals	Roots and tubers	Sugar (raw eq.)	Pulses (dry)	Vegetable oils, oilseeds (oil eq.)	Meat (carcass weight)	Milk and dairy (fresh milk eq.)
				kg/capita/year			
World							
1979-81	160	74	23.5	6.5	8.4	29.5	77
1997-99	171	69	24.0	5.9	11.4	36.4	78
2015	171	71	25.1	5.9	13.7	41.3	83
2030	171	74	26.3	6.1	15.8	45.3	90
Industrial countries							
1979-81	139	67	36.8	2.8	15.7	78.5	202
1997-99	159	66	33.1	3.8	20.2	88.2	212
2015	158	63	32.4	4.0	21.6	95.7	217
2030	159	61	32.0	4.1	22.9	100.1	221
Transition countries							
1979-81	189	119	45.9	3.1	9.2	62.9	181
1997-99	173	104	34.0	1.2	9.3	46.2	159
2015	176	102	35.0	1.2	11.5	53.8	169
2030	173	100	36.0	1.1	14.2	60.7	179
Developing countries							
1979-81	162	70	17.6	7.8	6.5	13.7	34
1997-99	173	67	21.3	6.8	9.9	25.5	45
2015	173	71	23.2	6.6	12.6	31.6	55
2030	172	75	25.0	6.6	14.9	36.7	66
Sub-Saharan Africa							
1979-81	115	172	9.9	9.8	8.5	10.6	34
1997-99	123	194	9.5	8.8	9.2	9.4	29
2015	131	199	11.3	9.8	10.7	10.9	31
2030	141	202	13.0	10.5	12.3	13.4	34
Near East and North Africa							
1979-81	199	26	28.2	6.4	11.1	17.4	85
1997-99	209	34	27.6	6.7	12.8	21.2	72
2015	206	33	28.7	6.9	14.4	28.6	81
2030	201	33	29.9	6.9	15.7	35.0	90
Latin America and Caribbean							
1979-81	130	74	48.5	12.6	10.2	40.6	97
1997-99	132	62	48.9	11.1	12.5	53.8	110
2015	136	61	48.2	10.7	14.5	65.3	125
2030	139	61	47.9	10.6	16.3	76.6	140
South Asia							
1979-81	151	20	20.7	11.2	5.8	4.0	42
1997-99	163	22	26.7	10.9	8.4	5.3	68
2015	177	27	29.5	9.1	11.6	7.6	88
2030	183	30	32.2	7.9	14.0	11.7	107
East Asia							
1979-81	181	83	8.1	4.3	4.7	13.0	5
1997-99	199	66	12.4	2.1	9.7	37.7	10
2015	190	64	14.6	2.0	13.1	50.0	14
2030	183	61	16.6	2.1	16.3	58.5	18

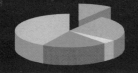

Table A5 Cereal balances

	Demand (million tonnes)			Production	Net trade	SSR[1] (%)		Growth rates (% per year)	
	Food	Feed	All uses					Demand	Production
World									
1979-81	706	575	1 437	1 442	3	100	1979-99	1.4	1.4
1997-99	1 003	657	1 864	1 889	9	101	1989-99	1.0	1.0
2015	1 227	911	2 379	2 387	8	100	1997-99 to 2015	1.4	1.4
2030	1 406	1 148	2 831	2 839	8	100	2015-2030	1.2	1.2
Industrial countries									
1979-81	110	286	428	551	111	129	1979-99	1.0	0.8
1997-99	142	331	525	652	111	124	1989-99	1.7	1.4
2015	150	387	599	785	187	131	1997-99 to 2015	0.8	1.1
2030	155	425	652	899	247	138	2015-2030	0.6	0.9
Transition countries									
1979-81	72	176	297	242	-41	81	1979-99	-1.9	-1.1
1997-99	72	105	211	210	1	100	1989-99	-4.9	-4.2
2015	70	127	237	247	10	104	1997-99 to 2015	0.7	1.0
2030	66	149	261	287	25	110	2015-2030	0.7	1.0
Developing countries									
1979-81	524	113	712	649	-66	91	1979-99	2.6	2.5
1997-99	790	222	1 129	1 026	-103	91	1989-99	2.2	2.1
2015	1 007	397	1 544	1 354	-190	88	1997-99 to 2015	1.9	1.6
2030	1 185	573	1 917	1 652	-265	86	2015-2030	1.5	1.3
Sub-Saharan Africa									
1979-81	40	2	48	41	-8	85	1979-99	3.4	3.4
1997-99	71	4	86	71	-14	82	1989-99	3.1	2.7
2015	116	8	139	114	-25	82	1997-99 to 2015	2.9	2.8
2030	173	15	208	168	-40	81	2015-2030	2.7	2.6
Near East and North Africa									
1979-81	47	19	80	58	-24	72	1979-99	2.7	2.4
1997-99	79	34	133	83	-49	63	1989-99	2.2	1.3
2015	107	62	192	107	-85	56	1997-99 to 2015	2.2	1.5
2030	131	93	249	133	-116	54	2015-2030	1.8	1.5
Latin America and Caribbean									
1979-81	46	37	94	87	-8	93	1979-99	2.3	1.8
1997-99	66	60	142	125	-14	88	1989-99	2.8	3.1
2015	85	98	204	188	-16	92	1997-99 to 2015	2.1	2.4
2030	99	135	257	244	-13	95	2015-2030	1.6	1.8
South Asia									
1979-81	134	2	151	147	-2	98	1979-99	2.6	2.7
1997-99	208	3	234	239	-3	102	1989-99	1.8	2.0
2015	295	11	335	323	-12	97	1997-99 to 2015	2.1	1.8
2030	360	22	416	393	-22	95	2015-2030	1.5	1.3
East Asia									
1979-81	257	53	339	316	-24	93	1979-99	2.5	2.5
1997-99	366	120	534	507	-23	95	1989-99	2.1	2.1
2015	404	218	675	622	-53	92	1997-99 to 2015	1.4	1.2
2030	422	309	787	714	-73	91	2015-2030	1.0	0.9

1 SSR = Self-sufficiency ratio = Production / total demand.

Table A6 Balances for selected commodities (million tonnes)

	Developing countries					Industrial countries					Transition countries				
	Demand					Demand					Demand				
	Food[1]	Feed	All uses	Production	Net trade	Food[1]	Feed	All uses	Production	Net trade	Food[1]	Feed	All uses	Production	Net trade
Wheat															
1979-81	171.8	7.5	205.1	156.8	-48.7	62.6	22.7	95.8	168.1	65.7	54.3	60.5	138.0	112.5	-15.7
1997-99	289.6	12.9	338.4	280.2	-61.8	75.3	52.1	142.3	215.9	66.0	56.1	28.1	101.8	100.8	-0.3
2015	392.3	27.7	461.8	358.1	-103.7	76.1	66.1	158.6	262.5	103.9	54.7	36.1	109.9	113.5	3.6
2030	478.1	41.2	566.0	424.9	-141.2	76.5	70.8	165.2	298.5	133.3	51.6	46.9	120.0	131.5	11.6
Rice (paddy)															
1979-81	333.1	5.8	370.8	368.7	-2.6	18.0	0.2	19.6	22.7	4.2	3.7	0.0	4.0	2.6	-1.7
1997-99	491.2	17.4	552.6	561.9	3.7	20.8	0.4	23.3	24.3	2.1	2.5	0.0	2.6	1.2	-1.4
2015	598.4	32.2	679.8	685.0	5.2	21.5	0.4	23.7	24.1	0.4	3.2	0.0	3.4	1.5	-1.9
2030	665.9	51.5	771.1	778.0	6.9	22.0	0.5	24.3	23.5	-0.8	3.5	0.0	3.8	2.0	-1.8
Coarse grains															
1979-81	130.4	102.1	259.5	246.5	-16.0	35.0	263.3	319.1	367.4	42.3	15.6	115.1	156.6	127.8	-24.5
1997-99	172.3	197.1	421.8	371.0	-43.2	52.8	278.1	367.1	420.3	43.4	13.8	76.5	107.2	108.6	2.1
2015	215.6	348.3	628.8	539.4	-89.4	59.9	320.8	423.9	506.7	82.8	13.1	90.4	124.9	133.0	8.1
2030	262.3	497.8	836.9	708.6	-128.2	64.0	353.7	470.7	585.3	114.6	12.1	102.5	139.0	153.9	14.9
Roots and tubers															
1979-81	227.1	62.5	339.9	356.4	16.4	52.4	30.6	99.6	83.3	-16.3	45.4	43.7	130.2	128.6	-0.3
1997-99	304.4	97.3	492.4	501.9	8.7	58.8	15.0	94.9	83.2	-11.5	43.0	26.2	98.0	94.9	-0.5
2015	412.4	142.6	653.2	662.9	9.6	59.6	15.6	98.1	86.6	-11.5	40.6	27.4	96.7	97.0	0.4
2030	513.8	182.2	808.2	817.6	9.4	59.6	15.7	99.9	88.3	-11.6	38.2	28.9	94.8	95.4	0.7
Sugar (raw eq.)															
1979-81	57.2	2.3	67.8	74.0	7.3	29.1	0.2	30.5	28.9	-2.0	17.5	0.9	18.8	12.8	-4.8
1997-99	97.2	3.9	121.9	128.8	5.8	29.5	0.1	31.6	36.0	3.8	14.1	0.4	15.2	8.6	-5.9
2015	135.4	6.0	167.3	173.0	5.7	31.5	0.1	33.8	36.9	3.1	13.9	0.5	15.2	9.9	-5.3
2030	171.4	8.2	208.5	212.0	3.5	32.3	0.1	34.6	38.7	4.1	13.7	0.5	15.1	10.9	-4.3
Pulses															
1979-81	25.3	2.6	31.8	31.5	-0.2	2.2	1.1	3.7	3.8	0.1	1.2	3.6	5.8	5.5	0.1
1997-99	31.0	4.7	40.5	39.3	-1.0	3.4	6.8	11.1	13.2	1.7	0.5	2.3	3.4	3.5	0.2
2015	38.3	7.4	51.9	51.0	-0.9	3.8	7.3	12.0	12.8	0.8	0.5	2.5	3.5	3.9	0.4
2030	45.4	10.5	63.5	62.4	-1.1	4.0	7.7	12.6	13.4	0.8	0.4	2.6	3.7	4.2	0.5
Vegetable oils, oilseeds (oil eq.)															
1979-81	21.0	0.5	26.4	28.6	1.5	12.3	0.5	17.0	17.2	-0.4	3.5	0.3	5.6	4.7	-0.9
1997-99	45.1	1.5	61.8	67.7	4.0	18.0	2.1	30.6	30.2	-0.9	3.8	0.5	6.0	5.8	-0.2
2015	73.2	2.4	105.7	109.1	3.4	20.6	2.4	40.9	40.4	-0.5	4.6	0.6	7.4	7.2	-0.2
2030	102.3	3.3	152.2	155.6	3.5	22.4	2.5	53.2	52.0	-1.3	5.4	0.6	9.1	9.2	0.0
Cocoa															
1979-81	0.2	0.0	0.3	1.7	1.3	1.1	0.0	1.1	0.0	-1.1	0.2	0.0	0.2	0.0	-0.2
1997-99	0.6	0.0	1.0	3.0	2.1	1.9	0.0	1.9	0.0	-1.8	0.4	0.0	0.4	0.0	-0.4
2015	1.0	0.0	1.4	4.1	2.7	2.2	0.0	2.3	0.0	-2.3	0.5	0.0	0.5	0.0	-0.5
2030	1.4	0.0	1.9	5.0	3.2	2.5	0.0	2.6	0.0	-2.6	0.6	0.0	0.6	0.0	-0.6
Coffee															
1979-81	1.5	0.0	1.6	5.3	3.5	3.3	0.0	3.3	0.0	-3.3	0.2	0.0	0.2	0.0	-0.2
1997-99	1.6	0.0	1.8	6.5	4.6	3.9	0.0	4.0	0.0	-4.0	0.5	0.0	0.5	0.0	-0.5
2015	2.5	0.0	2.7	7.8	5.2	4.5	0.0	4.5	0.0	-4.6	0.6	0.0	0.6	0.0	-0.6
2030	3.4	0.0	3.6	9.4	5.8	4.9	0.0	4.9	0.0	-5.2	0.8	0.0	0.8	0.0	-0.8

Table A6 Balances for selected commodities (million tonnes)(continued)

	Developing countries Demand Food¹	Feed	All uses	Production	Net trade	Industrial countries Demand Food¹	Feed	All uses	Production	Net trade	Transition countries Demand Food¹	Feed	All uses	Production	Net trade
Tea															
1979-81	1.4	0.0	1.4	1.9	0.5	0.5	0.0	0.5	0.1	-0.4	0.2	0.0	0.2	0.1	-0.1
1997-99	2.8	0.0	2.9	3.7	0.8	0.5	0.0	0.5	0.1	-0.4	0.3	0.0	0.3	0.1	-0.2
2015	4.1	0.0	4.2	5.1	0.9	0.6	0.0	0.6	0.1	-0.5	0.3	0.0	0.3	0.1	-0.3
2030	5.4	0.0	5.5	6.5	1.9	0.6	0.0	0.6	0.1	-0.5	0.4	0.0	0.3	0.1	-0.5
Beef and veal															
1979-81	15.1	0.0	15.2	15.7	0.5	22.7	0.0	22.8	22.8	0.1	8.8	0.0	8.9	8.7	-0.2
1997-99	27.8	0.0	28.1	28.0	-0.1	23.3	0.0	23.4	25.0	1.5	6.3	0.0	6.4	5.7	-0.6
2015	41.2	0.0	41.5	41.2	-0.3	24.6	0.0	24.7	26.6	1.9	7.0	0.0	7.1	6.3	-0.8
2030	55.3	0.0	55.7	55.0	-0.7	24.7	0.0	24.7	26.5	1.8	7.4	0.0	7.5	6.9	-0.6
Mutton and lamb															
1979-81	3.9	0.0	4.0	3.8	-0.2	2.0	0.0	2.1	2.5	0.4	1.2	0.0	1.2	1.2	0.0
1997-99	7.6	0.0	7.6	7.4	-0.3	2.2	0.0	2.3	2.7	0.4	0.7	0.0	0.8	0.8	0.0
2015	11.9	0.0	12.0	11.2	-0.7	2.2	0.0	2.3	3.1	0.8	0.9	0.0	1.0	0.9	0.0
2030	16.6	0.0	16.6	15.4	-1.2	2.2	0.0	2.3	3.5	1.3	1.1	0.0	1.1	1.1	0.0
Pig meat															
1979-81	17.1	0.0	17.4	17.5	0.1	23.7	0.0	23.8	23.7	-0.1	10.3	0.0	10.5	10.6	0.1
1997-99	49.4	0.0	49.5	49.3	-0.2	28.3	0.0	28.5	29.3	0.9	8.3	0.0	8.4	7.9	-0.5
2015	70.0	0.0	70.1	69.5	-0.6	31.2	0.0	31.3	32.3	0.9	8.5	0.0	8.5	8.4	-0.1
2030	83.5	0.0	83.6	82.8	-0.8	31.9	0.0	32.1	33.1	1.0	8.4	0.0	8.5	8.6	0.1
Poultry meat															
1979-81	8.2	0.0	8.3	7.7	-0.6	13.6	0.0	13.7	14.3	0.6	3.8	0.0	3.8	3.9	0.0
1997-99	31.5	0.0	31.9	31.3	-0.7	24.9	0.0	25.1	27.7	2.6	3.7	0.0	3.8	2.9	-0.9
2015	61.2	0.0	61.4	59.1	-2.3	33.0	0.0	33.1	37.5	4.3	5.0	0.0	5.1	4.1	-1.0
2030	96.5	0.0	96.7	93.5	-3.2	39.1	0.0	39.3	44.1	4.8	6.3	0.0	6.4	5.7	-0.6
Milk and dairy (fresh milk eq.)															
1979-81	110.2	12.7	129.5	112.3	-17.6	158.9	40.1	207.5	224.9	18.5	69.2	50.5	126.5	127.3	0.8
1997-99	203.7	23.2	239.1	219.3	-19.8	189.4	23.9	225.8	245.8	19.7	65.7	26.6	94.5	96.6	2.2
2015	322.8	36.4	375.8	346.2	-29.6	206.1	24.8	240.4	268.5	28.1	67.0	27.2	96.9	100.4	3.5
2030	451.8	50.8	523.1	484.0	-39.1	216.2	25.4	250.5	286.3	35.8	68.1	27.7	98.6	103.8	5.2
Cotton lint															
1979-81	8.3	0.0	8.3	8.2	-0.1	3.6	0.0	3.6	3.4	-0.2	2.6	0.0	2.6	2.7	0.1
1997-99	14.0	0.0	14.0	12.1	-1.7	3.9	0.0	3.9	4.8	0.9	0.8	0.0	0.8	1.5	0.7
2015	20.1	0.0	20.1	18.0	-2.1	4.5	0.0	4.5	6.0	1.5	1.0	0.0	1.0	1.7	0.7
2030	25.3	0.0	25.3	22.7	-2.5	4.8	0.0	4.8	6.9	2.0	1.2	0.0	1.2	1.8	0.6
Rubber															
1979-81	1.2	0.0	1.2	3.8	2.5	2.1	0.0	2.1	0.0	-2.1	0.4	0.0	0.4	0.0	-0.4
1997-99	3.3	0.0	3.2	6.6	3.4	3.1	0.0	3.1	0.0	-3.1	0.2	0.0	0.2	0.0	-0.2
2015	4.4	0.0	4.4	7.8	3.4	3.2	0.0	3.2	0.0	-3.2	0.3	0.0	0.3	0.0	-0.3
2030	5.4	0.0	5.4	8.9	3.5	3.2	0.0	3.2	0.0	-3.2	0.4	0.0	0.4	0.0	-0.4

1 Industrial use for cotton and rubber

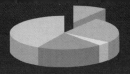

Table A7   Land use

	Arable land million ha			Harvested land million ha			Cropping intensity %		
	Total	Rainfed	Irrigated	Total	Rainfed	Irrigated	Total	Rainfed	Irrigated
Developing countries									
1997-99	956	754	202	885	628	257	93	83	127
2015	1 017	796	221	977	671	306	96	84	138
2030	1 076	834	242	1 063	722	341	99	87	141
Sub-Saharan Africa									
1997-99	228	223	5.3	154	150	4.5	68	67	86
2015	262	256	6.0	185	179	5.7	71	70	95
2030	288	281	6.8	217	210	7.0	76	75	102
Near East and North Africa									
1997-99	86	60	26	70	43	27	81	72	102
2015	89	60	29	77	45	32	86	75	110
2030	93	60	33	84	46	37	90	78	112
Latin America and Caribbean									
1997-99	203	185	18	127	112	16	63	60	86
2015	223	203	20	150	131	19	67	64	95
2030	244	222	22	172	150	22	71	68	100
South Asia									
1997-99	207	126	81	230	131	100	111	103	124
2015	210	123	87	248	131	117	118	106	134
2030	216	121	95	262	131	131	121	109	137
East Asia									
1997-99	232	161	71	303	193	110	130	120	154
2015	233	155	78	317	186	131	136	120	168
2030	237	151	85	328	184	144	139	122	169

Table A8   Yield and harvested land for selected crops

	Yield (tonnes/ha)				Harvested land (million ha)			
	1979-81	1997-99	2015	2030	1979-81	1997-99	2015	2030
Wheat								
Developing countries	1.64	2.53	3.11	3.53	95.6	110.7	113.3	118.4
Sub-Saharan Africa	1.30	1.62	2.03	2.44	1.0	1.6	2.2	2.8
Near East and North Africa	1.35	1.83	2.21	2.56	25.3	27.2	27.9	29.0
Latin America and Caribbean	1.50	2.53	2.84	3.17	10.1	8.9	9.5	10.5
South Asia	1.55	2.46	3.12	3.77	30.0	36.3	40.2	43.8
East Asia	2.04	3.15	3.99	4.30	29.1	36.7	33.5	32.2
Rice (paddy)								
Developing countries	2.65	3.57	4.21	4.73	138.0	156.7	162.1	163.9
Sub-Saharan Africa	1.36	1.63	2.19	2.79	4.5	7.1	8.6	10.1
Near East and North Africa	4.01	5.63	6.17	6.72	1.2	1.6	1.9	2.2
Latin America and Caribbean	1.94	3.47	4.35	4.91	8.0	5.9	6.4	6.9
South Asia	1.91	2.92	3.80	4.32	54.5	59.3	62.2	63.9
East Asia	3.36	4.17	4.67	5.23	70.0	82.8	83.0	80.8
Maize								
Developing countries	1.96	2.78	3.44	3.96	75.5	96.5	117.8	136.2
Sub-Saharan Africa	1.14	1.25	1.61	1.97	12.1	20.7	27.2	33.9
Near East and North Africa	2.39	4.66	5.29	6.39	2.3	2.2	2.6	3.2
Latin America and Caribbean	1.84	2.79	3.59	4.18	25.2	26.8	32.3	36.6
South Asia	1.14	1.68	2.25	2.72	7.1	8.0	8.5	8.8
East Asia	2.59	3.70	4.50	5.12	28.7	38.8	47.1	53.6
Barley								
Developing countries	1.29	1.42	1.74	2.05	16.6	16.9	18.2	19.6
Sub-Saharan Africa	1.21	1.06	1.34	1.65	0.9	1.0	1.2	1.4
Near East and North Africa	1.11	1.31	1.61	1.86	10.9	11.6	12.6	13.4
Latin America and Caribbean	1.36	1.87	2.51	3.04	0.9	1.0	1.3	1.8
South Asia	1.07	1.75	1.95	2.08	2.0	1.0	0.9	0.9
East Asia	2.70	1.79	2.18	2.64	1.8	2.3	2.2	2.2
Sugar cane								
Developing countries	54.9	61.8	77.4	88.1	12.4	18.7	20.5	22.0
Sub-Saharan Africa	56.8	49.5	62.8	75.0	0.6	0.9	1.2	1.5
Near East and North Africa	79.1	103.9	105.1	108.4	0.1	0.2	0.2	0.3
Latin America and Caribbean	57.3	64.7	76.0	82.8	6.2	8.5	8.9	9.3
South Asia	48.6	63.0	84.8	100.2	3.7	5.4	6.1	6.7
East Asia	56.9	54.7	71.5	83.6	1.8	3.8	4.0	4.2
Pulses								
Developing countries	0.61	0.67	0.85	1.09	51.8	60.0	59.7	57.1
Sub-Saharan Africa	0.55	0.44	0.66	0.93	7.8	15.8	17.4	18.4
Near East and North Africa	0.92	0.89	1.12	1.26	2.3	3.8	4.5	5.0
Latin America and Caribbean	0.58	0.84	0.98	1.06	8.3	7.3	7.3	7.8
South Asia	0.47	0.62	0.81	1.05	25.9	25.7	23.0	19.4
East Asia	1.07	1.04	1.15	1.54	7.6	7.4	7.5	6.6

Table A8 Yield and harvested land for selected crops (continued)

	Yield (tonnes/ha)				Harvested land (million ha)			
	1979-81	1997-99	2015	2030	1979-81	1997-99	2015	2030
Soybean								
Developing countries	1.37	1.84	2.24	2.63	21.2	40.8	56.5	71.5
Sub-Saharan Africa	0.56	0.85	1.11	1.40	0.4	0.8	1.2	1.7
Near East and North Africa	1.94	1.84	2.66	3.19	0.1	0.1	0.2	0.3
Latin America and Caribbean	1.66	2.33	2.74	3.15	11.2	21.6	30.7	39.7
South Asia	0.68	1.09	1.40	1.70	0.5	6.1	9.1	11.8
East Asia	1.08	1.41	1.83	2.21	9.0	12.1	15.2	18.0
Groundnut								
Developing countries	0.93	1.28	1.51	1.69	17.6	23.3	31.1	38.5
Sub-Saharan Africa	0.70	0.83	1.06	1.29	5.9	8.7	12.2	16.2
Near East and North Africa	1.76	2.42	2.85	3.23	0.1	0.1	0.2	0.2
Latin America and Caribbean	1.35	1.60	1.72	1.85	0.8	0.7	0.8	1.0
South Asia	0.84	1.03	1.27	1.43	7.2	7.4	8.7	9.5
East Asia	1.38	2.12	2.28	2.43	3.6	6.5	9.2	11.6
Seedcotton								
Developing countries	0.96	1.35	1.84	2.17	25.4	26.2	28.6	30.5
Sub-Saharan Africa	0.57	0.85	1.06	1.25	2.9	4.2	5.3	6.2
Near East and North Africa	2.12	2.70	2.93	3.10	1.6	1.6	2.2	2.6
Latin America and Caribbean	0.90	1.49	1.70	1.85	5.5	2.1	2.6	3.1
South Asia	0.61	0.91	1.54	2.08	10.1	12.1	12.8	13.1
East Asia	1.56	2.16	2.88	3.14	5.2	6.1	5.7	5.6
Rubber								
Developing countries	0.69	0.91	1.07	1.18	5.5	7.2	7.3	7.5
Sub-Saharan Africa	0.69	0.71	0.95	1.19	0.3	0.5	0.6	0.6
Near East and North Africa	0.00	0.00	0.00	0.00	0.0	0.0	0.0	0.0
Latin America and Caribbean	3.81	1.05	1.18	1.31	0.0	0.1	0.2	0.2
South Asia	0.67	1.20	1.34	1.50	0.4	0.6	0.6	0.6
East Asia	0.68	0.90	1.05	1.15	4.7	6.0	6.0	6.1

Sources

Given below is a list of sources for tables and figures only. A complete list of sources may be found in the main report.

Alexandratos, N. (ed.) 1988. *World agriculture towards 2000, an FAO study.* London: Belhaven Press, and New York, USA: New York University Press.

Alexandratos, N. (ed.) 1995. *World agriculture towards 2010, an FAO Study.* Chichester, UK: John Wiley and Sons, and Rome: FAO.

Anderson, K., François, J., Hertel, T., Hoekman, B. & Martin, W. 2000. Potential gains from trade reform in the new millennium. Paper presented at the Third Annual Conference on Global Economic Analysis, 27-30 June 2000, Monash University, Melbourne, Australia.

FAO. 1970. *Provisional indicative world plan for agricultural development.* Rome.

FAO. 1981. *Agriculture towards 2000.* Rome.

FAO. 2001. *Global forest resources assessment: main report.* FAO Forestry Paper 140. Rome.

FAO, forthcoming. *World agriculture towards 2015/30, an FAO study.* Rome.

Fischer, G., van Velthuizen, H. & Nachtergaele, F. 2000. *Global agro-ecological zones assessment: methodology and results.* Interim report. Laxenburg, Austria: International Institute for Systems Analysis (IIASA), and Rome: FAO.

Gallup, J., Sachs, J. & Mellinger, A. 1999. *Geography and economic development.* CID Working Paper No. 1. Harvard, USA: Harvard University.

Huang, J., Rozell, S., Pray, C. & Wang, Q. 2002. Plant biotechnology in China. *Science* 295: 674–677.

ISAAA. 2001. *Global preview of commercialised transgenic crops.* ISAAA Briefs Nos 21–24. Cornell, USA: Cornell University.

Mosier, A. & Kroeze, C. 1998. A new approach to estimating emissions of nitrous oxide from agriculture and its implications for the global change N20 budget. *IGBP Global Change Newsletter* 34: 8–13.

Oakridge National Laboratory. 2000. *Landscan global population density 2000 map.* Oak Ridge, USA.

Oldeman, L., Hakkeling, R. & Sombroek, W. 1991. World map of the status of human-induced soil degradation. Wageningen, Netherlands: ISRIC, and Nairobi: UNEP.

UN. 2001. *World population prospects: the 2000 revision: highlights.* New York, USA.

Willer, H. & Yussefi, M. 2002. *Organic agriculture worldwide 2001: statistics and future prospects.* Special publication. Stuttgart, Germany: Foundation for Ecology and Agriculture.

World Bank. 2001a. *World development indicators.* Washington DC.

World Bank. 2001b. *Global economic prospects and the developing countries, 2002.* Washington DC.

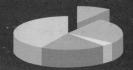

Acronyms

AIDS	acquired immunodeficiency syndrome
AoA	Agreement on Agriculture
BMI	body mass index
BSE	bovine spongiform encephalopathy
Bt	*Bacillus thuringensis*
EU	European Union
GDP	gross domestic product
GLASOD	Global Assessment of Land Degradation
GM	genetically modified
ha	hectare
HIV	human immunodeficiency virus
IPCC	Intergovernmental Panel on Climate Change
IPM	integrated pest management
IUCN	World Conservation Union
LDC	least developed country
MNE	multinational enterprise
NPK	nitrogen, phosphorus and potassium
NT/CA	no-till/conservation agriculture
NWFP	non-wood forest product
OECD	Organisation for Economic Co-operation and Development
ppm	parts per million
SFM	sustainable forest management
UN	United Nations
vCJD	variant Creutzfeldt-Jakob disease